Forward

by **Rufus Harrington**, Director of MSc Studies and
Senior Lecturer in CBT, University of Cumbria

Therapy has simple goals .... to enable us to better control our feelings and to change the way we think and behave, and so improve our lives. Acceptance Action Therapy (AAT) has proved to be a remarkably effective tool to achieve all these goals.

It is a pleasure for me to write a forward to this excellent book by the developer of this powerful therapy. I've known Graham for many years. I was his trainer and supervisor during his post-graduate 'Counselling Psychology' studies at Surrey University and then continued to be his clinical supervisor. I've trained many hundreds of psychologists and Cognitive Behavioural Psychotherapists and am the Director of MSc Studies in Cognitive Behavioural Therapy (CBT) at the University of Cumbria.

What I look for in a practicing psychologist, and in a therapy, is that they're effective in helping patients change their lives in real ways. What always impressed me about Graham, from the earliest days of his practice, was an independent turn of mind and a real ability to help his patients. I'm very results-orientated. I like to see patients get better. Graham achieves this. Furthermore, the techniques he's developed generate a significant further enrichment in patients' lives.

It's been my pleasure to watch and support Graham as he's developed his ideas and practice during the last decade. I've seen him qualify and practice and then develop his personal development trainings called 'Positive Mind Training', now available via webinars and attended by tens of thousands around the world.

Graham doesn't just use his ideas and techniques in therapy and teach them to others through development trainings. He and his clients live by them in their daily lives. As an experienced Cognitive Behavioural Therapy practitioner, I've come to use Graham's tools in my own work and have been hugely impressed by their simplicity and effectiveness. They can be used on their own or in combination with CBT or any other therapy. I'm also using the tools in my own life and, like so many others who've learned Graham's approaches, I'm finding them powerful and life-changing.

In my opinion, anyone interested in the workings of the human mind and how those workings can be enhanced .... and anyone interested in living a better life .... will benefit enormously from attending one of Graham's 'Positive Mind Training' development trainings (his webinars are now free or very low cost .... see www. abicord.com). Those interested in helping themselves or others to resolve emotional or behavioural problems, can attend the training and / or read this book.

Graham W Price

BPS, BABCP Acred, BACP, MBA, MSc

acceptance action therapy

A guide for therapists and anyone with a mind-based issue

Cover design by SpiffingCovers.com

Acceptance Action ideas, whether learned through Graham's development training, this book, or therapy, hugely enhance lives. Therapists and their clients will enjoy major benefits from participating in Graham's 'Positive Mind Training' webinars and / or reading this book, or by engaging in AAT.

Graham has developed AAT by supplementing some of the most modern, scientifically supported, principles of therapy and psychology. His work echoes themes to be found in CBT, Acceptance and Commitment Therapy (ACT) and Mindfulness approaches, all therapies having extensive scientific evidence to support their effectiveness. But Graham has built on these ideas and offers his own theory and a deceptively simple, elegant and effective way to apply that theory in practice. In my view his theory and practice are a major contribution to modern psychology and psychological therapy.

I like to see people living richer, happier more fulfilling lives. I see AAT patients becoming free of the psychological symptoms that imprison them. And I see them learning and applying Acceptance Action ideas to achieve better, more meaningful lives. Graham's 'Positive Mind Training' and / or this book, will enable you, or for therapists your patients, to do the same.

Rufus Harrington
Consultant Cognitive Behavioural Psychologist
Director of MSc Studies and Senior Lecturer in CBT,
University of Cumbria

About the Author

Graham W Price is a Chartered Psychologist, psychotherapist, practicing member of the British Psychological Society (BPS) and accredited member of the British Association for Behavioural and Cognitive Psychotherapies (BABCP).

His therapy practice focuses on Acceptance Action Therapy (AAT), his own creation and the subject of this book, incorporating some aspects of Cognitive Behavioural Therapy (CBT). He is also trained and qualified in psychodynamic therapy, hypnotherapy, humanist approaches, neuro linguistic programming (NLP) and other therapies, which he occasionally uses to support his core approach.

He is also a personal and executive coach, personal development trainer, stress-management consultant, relationships counsellor/coach/trainer, weight loss and smoking cessation specialist and professional speaker. He has developed a personal development version of AAT called Acceptance Action Training, which he uses in his coaching, development trainings (called Positive Mind Training), relationships work, weight management and smoking cessations.

The tools are so effective that where results can easily be measured and evidenced, such as smoking cessation (99% sustained success to date, more recently 100%) and weight loss (95% sustained success to date, more recently 98%), he provides a one year money-back guarantee for achieving goals and sustaining them.

He presents AAT and Acceptance Action Training to the public through his 'psychology and development services' company, Abicord, and to organisations through Abicord Consulting.

As a quantifiable illustration of the effectivenesss of AAT, Graham's 95% sustained success for weight loss compares with under 10% for other internationally-very-well-known programmes and his 99% sustained success for smoking cessation compares with below 40% for other well known approaches.

Graham is a Neuro-Linguistic Programming (NLP) Master Practitioner and Certified Trainer. AAT and Acceptance Action Training contain no NLP, though NLP does briefly mention, though rarely uses, a variation of the 'determinist' principle of AAT. Graham provides NLP trainings to organisations if requested, though he and his clients have found that Acceptance Action Training is significantly more impactful, effective and sustained.

Preface

I consider myself very fortunate. Many years ago (I don't care to think how many) I became interested in personal development. Through a parallel study of Eastern philosophy, I developed an interest in the concept of 'acceptance', a core principle of Eastern philosophy.

I was introduced to the principle of 'accepting what is' by an executive in the corporate world where I worked at the time. I describe that experience in my on-line development webinar called Positive Mind Training.

I developed the technique that became known as 'Positive Acceptance' as a means of training myself to 'accept what is' more of the time and, eventually, all of the time. The term 'Positive Acceptance' was later shortened to 'Pacceptance'. I never imagined back then what an influence this concept, and its many applications and ramifications, would have on my own life and the lives of thousands of others.

I was so impressed with the impact on my life, that I took a year off work to think about life and the possibilities for personal change. I spent a great deal of time thinking about thinking.

During that time, I developed the ideas that later became known as Acceptance Action Training and Acceptance Action Therapy (AAT). I became a counsellor, subsequently taking a psychology degree followed by post-graduate training to become a Chartered Psychologist.

After I was introduced to the concepts of 'accepting what is', accepting feelings and 'determinist thinking', all outlined in this book, and had further developed those ideas, it was a while before I had the confidence to start using them in counselling and therapy. I assumed that while they worked amazingly well in my own life, there was no reason to believe they'd be easily transferable to others, particularly as some of the ideas can seem quite radical to those hearing them for the first time.

My assumption was wrong. As soon as I started using them with my clients, I could see how easily they were adopting them and what a difference it was making in their lives.

Years later, I attended a weekend workshop by one of the world's leading development trainers. Despite teaching excellent material, as far as I can recall he never mentioned the word 'acceptance', never mind the concept of 'accepting what is'. I was amazed. In my view an ability to 'accept what is' is by far the most valuable attribute we can develop in our lifetime and considerably more than half of what a satisfying and successful life is about.

In my training as a psychologist and psychotherapist, the term 'acceptance' was occasionally mentioned, particularly in the context of Rational Emotive Behaviour

Therapy (REBT), Acceptance and Commitment Therapy (ACT) and, much later, Mindfulness. But there was never any mention of the concept of 'accepting what is'.

This seemed to me a significant deficiency in the whole field of personal development, therapy and therapy training. So I started my own trainings, initially called 'The Power to Choose', teaching Positive Acceptance (later renamed Pacceptance) and the various techniques derived from this principle. Later, after others adopted the name 'Power to Choose' for a range of trainings, some religious, and even promotion of an electricity company, I changed the name to 'Positive Mind Training'.

The purpose of this book is to help therapists use these ideas and techniques in therapy and to help those with emotional and behavioural problems to help themselves.

Research to date has shown that AAT is substantially more effective than any other therapy. That research is outlined at the end of this book.

I wish you all the benefits I've had the good fortune to enjoy in using these tools, both in your own life and, if you're a therapist or coach, for the benefit of your clients

Graham W Price
BPS, HCPC, BABCP Accredited, MBA, MSc

Contents

Introduction

Have you ever wondered how you might choose to think and behave if we had the ability to make that choice, all the time?

Perhaps you'd choose to be super confident, highly achieving and successful. Maybe you'd choose to be a free spirit, develop your talents and lead a life of passion. Perhaps you'd choose to focus on relationships, revel in your freedom and enjoy life to the full. Or would you see your role as one of contribution, creating a better world, making your life and the lives of your family and others more satisfying and fulfilling? Perhaps you'd choose all those things.

The key question isn't what we'd choose. The more important question is … why aren't we already exercising that choice? Is it because we don't have the ability to? Or is it because we don't realise, or don't believe, that we have that ability?

Most of us have at least some limitations in our abilities and self-beliefs and hence in the ways we think and behave. We're not born with these limitations. We develop them, partly through the influence of our culture, our elders and our experience, but primarily, as we'll see in this book, through our behaviour. But the process by which we developed them can be reversed. The role of therapy and coaching is to contribute to that reversal.

How much time have you spent in your life thinking about who you are, who you'd like to be, what limitations might be preventing you from crossing that divide and what you'd need to do to unwind those limitations and make your life amazing? If you're a therapist or coach, perhaps the same question could be asked of your clients.

By my mid-20s the amount of time I'd spent thinking about these things was probably zero. I'd been doing what most people spend most of their lives doing. Living on auto pilot. Living life the best way I knew how. Trying to make the most of the opportunities that life presents. Dealing with and coping with and sometimes struggling with, the challenges that life throws in our path. Allowing life's experiences to create the skills, abilities and limitations that naturally arise from those experiences.

Had I ever thought about consciously intervening in, and taking control of, this process? No. Had I ever thought it might be possible to do so? No. Had the culture I grew up in (a British middle class culture), or my education, ever encouraged me to think about these things? No.

Around that time I had a stroke of good fortune. I learned something that, for the first time, gave me one ability to take control of the way I thought. I'll share that learning with you in Chapter 1. That in turn caused me, for the first time, to take stock of my life. What I saw didn't please me greatly. The summary, as I recall, was ... career: fair; self-confidence and self-belief: poor; satisfying lasting relationships: poor.

I decided to do something about taking control of my life. As mentioned in the preface, I took time out to think about life. I did a lot of thinking, reading, listening and challenging my thoughts and behaviour. The result was a massive change. I became much more confident, acquired much greater self-belief, developed new abilities, removed limitations and took control of my thinking, feelings, behaviour and my life.

These changes initially drove development of my corporate career and later a change of profession to becoming a psychologist. Still later they led me to develop a life-skills training and a new therapy.

The life-skills training, 'Acceptance Action Training', is available on line under the title 'Positive Mind Training'. The therapy is the subject of this book.

Note to Therapists and Coaches

If you're a therapist or coach I have some advice for you. I recommend you spend some time integrating the personal development ideas contained in the first half of this book, or my more extensive on-line development training, Positive Mind Training, into your own life, before you try using them in therapy or coaching for the benefit of your clients.

AAT is different from most therapies. The ideas contained in AAT and Acceptance Action Training have such broad application, they can, and inevitably will, be used by therapists and coaches as personal development tools to enhance their own lives, whether or not they have any issues of their own.

There are no AAT techniques that are only useful for resolving emotional or behavioural problems. Every aspect can usefully be applied to anyone's life, both day to day and in dealing with the periodic challenges we all face from time to time.

It's possible to learn techniques used in some practical therapies and use them as a therapist without having experienced them yourself. We don't need to have used a 'Thought Record' on ourselves in order to use this tool as a CBT therapist. This is not the case with AAT.

I suggest you need to have used AAT principles and techniques in your own life before you can teach them competently as a therapist or coach. How long is up to you. I'd suggest a minimum of a month or two.

1

Resistance is Futile

Almost all emotional or behavioural problems result from a combination of 'resistance' and unproductive action. In this context, 'resistance' means having negative thoughts about something, either consciously or unconsciously. In other words resistance means 'wanting something to be different'.

If I'm unhappy, dissatisfied, stressed, distressed, anxious, depressed or worried, I'm resisting something. I may be resisting some aspect of my life right now. I may be resisting past events. Or, in the case of worry, I'm resisting the future.

And if this resistance results in me experiencing uncomfortable feelings (in this book 'feelings' means the same as 'emotions') and I'm not happy about experiencing those feelings, then I'm resisting my feelings. (This will be addressed in Chapter 3).

All resistance is irrational. If I'm resisting the past, then I'm wanting the past to be different. Quite probably I'm wanting something that's happened not to have happened. Clearly the past cannot be changed. So I'm wishing for the impossible.

The same is true of resisting the present. If I'm having negative thoughts about something in the present, then I'm wanting a current situation, or something that's happening right now, to be different. Things can only ever be changed in the next moment or the future. We can never undo 'what already is'. To do that we'd need a time machine to take us back in time so we can revisit the present and change it. So wanting the present to be different is also wishing for the impossible.

We could call resisting the past 'resisting what was' and resisting the present 'resisting what is', but in AAT we combine them in the single term 'resisting what is', which means wanting something to be 'already different'. 'Resisting what is' is always wishing for the impossible. Examples of 'resisting what is' are regret, being dissatisfied or stressed by a current situation; wanting to be healthier, wealthier or more confident right now or complaining (unproductively) about others.

Accepting what is:

The opposite of resistance is acceptance. The opposite of 'resisting what is', we call 'accepting what is'. This means accepting the past or present, i.e. stop wishing things were 'already' different.

Traditional wisdom:

'Accepting what is' is different from our usual meaning of 'acceptance'. In our culture 'acceptance' is generally seen to mean 'letting things be'. This is often seen as weak as we'd rather change things or make them better.

It makes sense, however, to 'accept things we cannot change'. This is reflected in 'traditional' wisdom on acceptance, often called the Serenity Creed, which says 'Accept the things we cannot change; change the things we can change'.

This distinction between the things we can or cannot change is 'future' oriented, since we can only change or not change something in the future. By contrast 'accepting what is' is about accepting the past or present.

For most people, the idea of 'accepting things we cannot change' is not particularly useful. In my case I cannot recall any issue I've ever had that I didn't think I should be able to do something about. So my issues all fell into the category of 'Change the things we can change'. So the concept of 'acceptance' addressed by the Serenity Creed, was of little use to me. Yet 'accepting what is' applies to everything.

Research on resistance:

Before explaining how we can reduce or eliminate resistance, I'll outline some research we've carried out. Our studies have shown that the average person has around 20 resistant thoughts per day. These are mostly minor, but from time to time, we may experience more major resistant thoughts.

Those seeking therapy may be having significantly more such thoughts than the average person and more of those resistant thoughts may well be major.

On average around 90% of resistant thoughts involve wanting the past or present to be different and the other 10% involve resisting the future, i.e. worry.

We watched 10 minutes of East Enders (a daily UK TV drama) and counted 87 resistant thoughts. That translates to one every 7 seconds or around 4,000 per day for a typical East Enders character. As it's a drama it's perhaps hardly surprising that this number is high, but I've helped clients who get pretty close.

Positive Acceptance

Once these ideas became clear to me, I developed, with some colleagues, a four step process to reduce 'resisting what is' in our lives and develop our ability to 'accept what is'. This process later became known as Positive Acceptance.

1. Create a habit of noticing whenever we're resisting what is (wanting the past or present to be different).
2. Acknowledge this is an irrational thought (for the reasons I've given).
3. Drop the resistant thought. (This may sound challenging but once the first two steps have been carried out, it's surprisingly easy).
4. Refocus on what we can do, if anything, to improve the future.

Some supplementary points:
- Start with minor situations then, after some practice, e.g. a few days, apply it to everything.
- Step 3 'dropping the resistant thought' isn't about trying to suppress thoughts. Trying to suppress

negative thoughts isn't generally helpful as it may just result in strengthening them. Dropping them is about gently letting them go.

- The thought may come back. Initially that will happen a lot. Think of this as a bonus. Positive Acceptance needs practice. If the thought comes back, that's just another opportunity to practice. Keep applying the process until the thought stops returning. Don't just repeat step 3. Go back to step 2.
- Most of the time, step 4 isn't needed. We may not be able to think of anything useful to do or the situation may not be significant enough to warrant doing anything
- Once we're familiar with the process, we can drop step 2 and reduce it to a 3-step process. As most of the time step 4 isn't needed it becomes mostly a 2-step process (steps 1 and 3).
- After a short while the process becomes more automatic. We find we're 'accepting what is' most of the time.
- Step 3 is equivalent to 'accepting what is'. So Positive Acceptance is a combination of 'accepting what is' and, where appropriate, taking action to improve the future.

The rationale for 'accepting what is' that I've provided so far is that it's too late to change the past or present. The limitation of this rationale is that it doesn't deal effectively with blame: either self-blame or blaming others. I may know I can't undo what's happened or 'what is' but I may still be thinking it should have been different. "I shouldn't have done what I did" or "they shouldn't have done what they did." There's a more powerful rational for 'accepting what is' that eliminates blame. I'll introduce this in the next chapter.

When I started giving Acceptance Action Trainings, I found the term Positive Acceptance too lengthy, particularly if used as a verb. So I took the 'P' out of Positive and placed it on the front of Acceptance creating the word **Pacceptance**. (The P is pronounced as in Pack and the remainder as in acceptance)

There are tens of thousands of development training participants and therapy clients using Pacceptance every day in their lives.

Worry

I've mentioned that, on average, around 10% of resistant thoughts are about resisting the future, i.e. worry. Worry is also irrational. When we're worrying, we have a negative image of something that will or 'might' happen in the future, that we don't want to happen. But when we're worrying, we also believe we cannot control whatever we're worrying about. If we believed we could control it, we wouldn't be worrying.

Wanting something to be different in the future that we believe we cannot control is as irrational as wanting the past to be different. (We have no control over that either). It also ignores the wisdom of the Serenity Creed.

The only productive things to do if we find ourselves worrying are:

a) Do whatever we can do to gain more control
b) To the extent that we cannot do a), 'accept whatever will be'

A powerful illustration of this 'acceptance' approach to worry is the well-known song 'Que (pronounced 'kay') sera sera; whatever will be will be', sung by Doris Day in the 1950s. The song responds to worries about the future with this simple statement … 'Whatever will be will be'. This implies that we need to accept whatever will be if we cannot control it. This doesn't mean we shouldn't do whatever we can to improve the future. But it's clearly a wise response when we find ourselves worrying about any aspect of life that we cannot control.

In fact the expression 'Whatever will be will be' doesn't just apply to things we cannot control. It applies to everything. In areas we can control, we'll do whatever we can do, and are willing to do, to improve the future, and once that's happened the result will still be 'whatever it will be'. That doesn't mean it's already determined or predictable; it just means that when the future arrives, it will be whatever it will be.

I suggest to all my clients that they use the expression 'whatever will be will be' whenever they find themselves worrying, until it becomes embedded in their natural way of thinking.

The four step process for worry (equivalent to the four step Pacceptance tool already described) becomes:

1. Create a habit of noticing whenever we're worrying
2. Acknowledge that this is irrational (as irrational as wanting the past to be different)
3. Drop the worrying thought (and replace it with 'Que sera sera; whatever will be will be' … accepting that whatever that may be, we'll be able to cope with it.)
4. Refocus on what we can do, if anything, to gain more control of whatever we were worrying about

I personally used to be a prolific worrier. I completely eliminated worry from my life in a few weeks by repeatedly using this tool until it became my natural way of thinking.

If the worry is major, accepting that 'whatever will be will be' can sometimes seem unrealistic. In that case I recommend starting with another tool concerning exaggeration.

When we're worrying, we're almost always exaggerating either (or both of) the probability of something negative happening, or the consequences even if it were to happen. When in my youth I used to feel anxious speaking to groups, I'd worry about an upcoming presentation. I was certainly exaggerating both the probability of a disaster occurring (I'd already survived a number of presentations) and the consequences even if something did go wrong (I think I imagined life would end as I knew it). Someone with a fear of flying is certainly exaggerating the probability of a disaster occurring, but perhaps not the consequences if it were to occur.

So if we find ourselves with a major worry, it would pay us to think about what we're exaggerating. That puts the worry into a more reasonable perspective. We can then apply the 'whatever will be will be' tool to eliminate the worry.

Another AAT approach to worry is to recognise that once we've practiced Pacceptance and found we can Paccept any situation, or any event that's happened, we'll know that whatever happens in the future, we'll be able to Paccept it.

This last approach is only useful once we've become reasonably skilled at Pacceptance. But I find that clients can quickly become sufficiently skilled at Pacceptance that they can soon see the sense of this approach with regard to worrying and successfully apply it.

I can recall from my own experience that I used to think that suffering a major disability would be hugely challenging to cope with. Within a few weeks of starting to practice Pacceptance, that belief changed. I became confident that whatever happened to me, I'd be able to Paccept it.

Summary

We eventually broadened the definition of Pacceptance to include dealing with worry. So Pacceptance became accepting the past, present and future while taking action to improve the future wherever this is possible and warranted.

I chose to get tough with myself. I refused to allow myself to maintain a resistant thought, whether I was resisting the past, present or future, on the grounds that all resistance is irrational. I recommend my clients follow the same approach. Once the more powerful Pacceptance tool outlined in the next chapter is added, together with 'accepting feelings' outlined in the following chapter, most of my clients succeed in eliminating, or significantly diminishing, all forms of resistance from their lives.

2.

An Extraordinary Truth

I mentioned in the preface to this book, that I was initially concerned that some aspects of AAT could be seen as radical and that my clients might find them hard to understand and accept. I then said this hasn't proved to be the case. My clients may initially be surprised by the contents of this chapter, but 'hard to understand and accept'? Not at all.

Practically all those that I've shared it with, which means all those for whom it's relevant in resolving an issue, have understood and accepted it straight away and then used it extensively in resolving their issue and subsequently in removing resistant thoughts from their lives. I trust the same will be true for you as you read the extraordinary truth that I'm about to share with you.

The determinist principle

Everything that you, or I, or anyone else has ever thought, felt or done at every moment of our lives is the only thing we could possibly have thought, felt or done at that moment.

Surprising though this may sound, the explanation is remarkably simple. We live in a 'determined' world.

This means that everything we've ever thought, felt or done was totally determined by just two things. The first was our situation at the time. The second was 'who we were' at that moment. Who we are at any moment is made up of a long list of things including our attitudes or ways we've learned to think, our beliefs (conscious and unconscious), our morals and values, our knowledge and abilities, our strengths and weaknesses, our unconscious programming and a bunch of other current attributes or limitations.

You might be thinking you can see how all these things might influence how we think, feel and behave, but surely we still have choice, at least in what we do. You might, for example, be thinking you were who you were at mid-day yesterday, but you still had a choice whether to get on the bus or not get on the bus.

We certainly do have choice. Indeed we make hundreds of choices every day. But the key question isn't whether we have a choice. The key question is: why did we make the choice we made? The answer is always: because of our situation and who we were at that moment.

Could we have made a different choice? No. We'd need to have been a slightly different person with some slightly different attribute and hence a slightly different way of thinking.

This isn't saying things were 'fated' to happen. But it is saying they're the only thing that could have happened at each moment, given who we were at that moment.

Our history

Why are we who we are at any moment? We're always a product of our entire life history up to any moment. So the only way we could have been a different person and hence thought, felt or done something different, is if we'd had a slightly different history. At any moment that clearly wasn't possible. But as time moves on, we keep changing as a result of new events and experiences that add to our history. So our choices in the present or future may be different to our choices in the past, even in an identical situation.

Furthermore our history at any moment is the only history we could possibly have had. After all, our history is made up of things we, and others who've influenced us, have done. And all of those people were doing the only thing they could have done, given who they were, at every moment.

The philosophy

All of this is the realm of philosophy. All philosophers know we live in a determined world. Philosophers call this 'determinism'. AAT calls it 'determinist thinking'.

Very few others, including very few psychologists, know this truth. The section at the beginning of this book called 'About the Author', mentions that Neuro Linguistic Programming (NLP) has a similar principle, but it's little used and its full significance is little understood in the world of NLP.

Philosophers used to debate this issue. But those debates ended many decades ago. There simply wasn't anyone left in the world of philosophy who could put together a convincing argument against determinism. There are still arguments about peripheral issues, and about our ability to exercise 'free choice' (described in philosophy as "free will"), but not about the basic principles relating to the past, that I've so far outlined.

To allay any fears you might have that this means we have no real freedom to choose our future, I should tell you right away that philosophers only apply full determinism to the past. The future is wide open to make whatever we want, and are able, to make, as we've always known it to be.

The present is a mixed bag. We apply the determinist principle to others in the present, in other words they're all doing the only thing they could be doing right now, but not necessarily to ourselves, for reasons I'll come to.

I've spoken to many philosophers and read a great deal about what they say. I've never come across anyone who understands the subject who argues against it. You can put the name of Bertrand Russell, probably the world's best known philosopher, or Albert Einstein, probably the world's best known scientist, into a search engine, together with the word 'determinism' and see what they say.

Einstein lived when this topic was still being debated. He understood, and fully agreed with, determinism. But the intriguing thing about him was that he got irritated with people who didn't understand it and were still arguing against it. That says to me that he didn't totally understand determinism. If he had, he'd have known that those who didn't fully understand it, and were arguing against it, were doing the only thing they could possibly have been doing.

The benefits so far

The immediate benefits of 'determinist thinking' are huge. It removes regret, guilt, self-blame and blaming others. It invalidates blaming statements such as 'I or we or they, should have done something different, or shouldn't have done whatever we did'. The word 'should' implies a 'could'. In a determined world, the expression 'could have' is invalid, so 'should have' is invalid too (unless it's just being used constructively in the sense of lessons learned to guide future behaviour).

'Determinist thinking' gives us a more powerful rationale to 'Paccept' everything that's happened, whether that relates to things we've done or things others have done. AAT calls this the 'determinist rationale' for Pacceptance. The rationale I provided in Chapter 1 (it's too late to change the past or the present) is called the 'time-based' rationale. You'll recall I pointed out that the 'time-based' rationale doesn't deal effectively with blame, whereas the determinist rationale does. Which basis I give to a client (if I cover Pacceptance at all) will depend on their issue, as we'll see when we look at case examples.

Responsibility

The Professor of Philosophy who first explained to me the principles of determinism, gave an intriguing answer to my question "why have I never been told, until now, that we live in a determined world?" He explained that if philosophers publicised the fact that everything we've ever done is the only thing we could have done, that would give a wonderful 'cop out' to all the bad people who've done bad things. He surmised we'd have bank robbers walking into court with their philosopher, saying to the judge and jury "listen to this guy; he'll tell you that robbing the bank was the only thing I could have done." And indeed that would be true. It isn't difficult to understand that he robbed the bank because of his selfish and immoral 'bank robber' ways of thinking.

But I disagreed with the professor on his concern about a 'cop out'. It seemed to me that even in a determined world, we're still responsible for what we do or what we've done. But that responsibility becomes primarily about what we do now and in the future, in relation to things we've already done. What we've done may be the only thing we could have done, given who we were at the time, but we still need to decide what we're going to do 'now forward' in relation to any negative things we may have done in the past. Are we going to repeat the behaviour or change it? Are we going to apologise, or make amends, to others we may have hurt? And of course 'responsibility' includes whatever penalties or other consequences others or society may meat out in response to what we've done?

So the judge in the professor's example, if familiar with determinism, might say to the bank robber "I know that robbing the bank was the only thing you could have done, given your 'bank robber' mentality, self-justifications and attitudes you had at the time. But in our society we have rules, and consequences for breaking those rules, so you're still going to prison. And while you're there I suggest you take responsibility for what you've done by thinking about what you're going to do when you come out of prison and how you might contribute better to society and to others in the future".

Clearly society's rules, moral values and potential consequences are part of the 'situation' that contributes to our attitudes and behaviour much of the time. We might surmise that if we didn't have those rules, values and consequences there might be more people selfishly robbing banks.

Philosophers and psychologists inhabit different worlds. Philosophers know about determinism but seem to rarely apply it to their own lives. Psychologists generally know little about determinism, unless they're familiar with AAT, and so aren't aware that they and their clients have always thought, felt and acted in the only way they could possibly have thought, felt and acted at every moment, and that regret, guilt and blame therefore have no validity. But once psychologists and other therapists learn about AAT and determinist thinking, they generally quickly understand the value of this knowledge to both themselves and their clients.

The determinist paradox

We're saying the past is always the only thing it could have been but the future is wide open. This seems to create a paradox as, when we get to the future and look back, once again the past is the only thing it could have been. Philosophers provide two explanations or 'solutions' for this paradox, one relatively weak, the other powerful.

The weaker explanation arises from the science of Quantum Mechanics, which says, among other things, that the behaviour of electrons is not predictable. Random events are happening at a sub-atomic level all the time. (This has now been verified by experiments with sub-atomic particles in 'accelerometers'). Therefore there are random elements in our thoughts and actions. That understanding removed 'pure' determinism, which had previously said the future was predictable and therefore already 'laid out in the sand'. Pure determinists believed in 'fate'. Quantum mechanics removed that concept. But when we look at the past, random events have already happened and in the presence of those random 'outcomes', the past is still the only thing it could have been. Future random events haven't yet happened so the future is clearly not predictable. But the existence of random events still doesn't put us in control of our future.

The second explanation is much more powerful, and gives us the ability to exercise genuine "free will" and so take full control of our future. It can be explained this way. If I say "I acted foolishly yesterday, but that's the only thing I could have done given who I was at the time", that would be true (and enables me to feel better about the foolish thing that I've done). But if I say "I'm acting foolishly right now and that's the only thing I could be doing, given who I am right now", that clearly wouldn't be true because, if I'm aware of what I'm doing right now, I can snap out of it. So self-awareness in the present moment can enable me to freely choose my actions and so take control, despite the determinist principle.

This can alternatively be described this way. We're all on 'auto pilot' most of the time. (For many people, that may be all of the time for our whole lives). This means we're just thinking and acting in the way that 'who we are' is driving us to think and act right now. The only way we can escape from this is to become aware of our auto pilot; in other words to become aware of the patterns that are driving our thinking and behaviour. Then, and only then, can we break free of those patterns, and freely choose what we do.

AAT is at least partly about giving ourselves, and our clients, the tools to become aware of our patterns, break free from them and freely choose our future.

So with sufficient insight, we can take control of the application of determinism to ourselves in the present moment. Hence we apply determinist thinking completely to the past, to others in the present (me understanding that others are driven by their auto pilot right now, and so are doing the only thing they could be doing, doesn't give them the awareness to break their patterns), but not necessarily to ourselves in the present. If we're aware of our auto pilot, and are willing and able to break away from it, we can freely choose what we do. And as we'll find out, doing this repeatedly is the way to change our auto pilot, in other words is the way to change the mind-set that will drive the way we think and behave in future.

You may be thinking that if we can choose freely in the present moment, why couldn't we have done so yesterday? The simple answer is that if we could have done, we would have done. But we didn't, so clearly we didn't have the awareness to do so at that moment. So the past is always fully determined and is always the only thing it could have been.

If you're trying right now to challenge all of this, I have a suggestion. Rather than trying to out-think the philosophers, who've spent decades thinking through all of this and developing the current philosophy of determinism, we might be better to focus for now on applying the huge benefits that 'determinist thinking' offers in relation to Paccepting the past and Paccepting what others are doing right now, and to taking control of our future.

Taking control

So one major strength of determinist thinking lies in the present moment. This is where the possibility of change exists. We can think about our unproductive patterns beforehand. We can realise the possibility for change beforehand. We can plan for change beforehand. But real change can only happen now.

That change may require understanding that only in the present moment can we truly make a free choice. It may require prior commitment. It may require determination. It may require courage. But the possibility for change always exists. It's up to us whether we choose to make it happen. The means to create that change is the subject of the next chapter.

Accepting ourselves

Who we are right now is the only person we could possibly have been right now. After all, who we are is always a product of our entire history up to this moment. And we've already said that in a determined world our history couldn't possibly have been different. So who we are right now couldn't possibly have been different either. Your or your client's issues, health, wealth, weight, shape, attitudes, beliefs, strengths, weaknesses and character right now are unquestionably the only thing they could have been. Knowing this aids self-acceptance and accepting others. But this doesn't stop us doing whatever we need to do to become who we want to be in the future.

Film analogy

When I think a client has grasped the truth of determinist thinking, I may enhance their understanding of its significance by describing an analogy with a movie.

When we're watching a movie we don't tend to suggest the contents of the movie should somehow be different. That's because we realise that what we're seeing on the screen is the only thing that could be happening. After all the script writer, director and actors have put it there. Furthermore it's on the DVD in the projector room so we know that, for all these reasons, what we're watching on the screen couldn't possibly be different.

Well life is the same. OK, it's not pre-determined in the way a movie is. It's not been written by a script writer or directed by a director. And it's not on a DVD in a projector room. But it is the only thing that could possibly be happening, given who everyone is right now. So there's no more reason to think it could or should be different than if we were watching it on a movie.

And when we've finished watching the movie, we don't tend to think that what we've seen should have been different. Life again is the same. Everything that's already happened in life is the only thing that could possibly have happened, given who everyone was at each moment.

So in a 'determined' world, there's no more reason to think that life could or should have been different from the way it was, or that it could or should be different from the way it is, than if we were watching it on a movie. In life, the script is determinism. The director is everyone's auto pilot.

But there is one big difference between life and watching a movie. When we're watching a movie we don't have the ability to climb into the movie and influence what's happening. Perhaps one day that technology might exist. Perhaps one day everyone in the audience will have their own version of the movie that they watch on their own 'virtual reality' monitor. Perhaps we'll each be able to become part of our movie and change what happens. All the other actors will be doing what the script writer and director have told them to do, unless we change it directly through our influence. With that technology, I imagine movies will become hugely more exciting. I imagine cinemas will dramatically expand. Audiences will flock to them to take part.

We already have this technology. It's called life. In life everyone is doing the only thing they could be doing all the time unless we change it. They're following a determined script. (Not a pre-determined script but a script that's evolving moment by moment in a determined way). In life, the only person who's in a position to change the script is us. In life everything that's happening in our world is following a script, moment by moment, unless we choose to change the script. Not only can we change what we do but, to a lesser extent, we can influence what others do too. We can change our script, and we can influence their script.

That makes life as amazing as the high-tech movie I've described. The only mistake we make is thinking the script could or should be different without us taking action to change it. The mistake we make is thinking our script and our current limitations, or the other actors' script and their limitations should be different, unless we take action to change them.

Furthermore if we simply continue to take action on auto pilot, we'll continue to be part of the script, totally determined by the script writer (determinism) and the director (our auto pilot). But if we're willing to break out of our auto pilot, if we're willing to act powerfully with full awareness of our freedom to do so, then we're able to write our own script. We're able to create the movie of our choosing.

Making a powerful choice

When explaining determinist thinking, I'm often asked how can we know if we're acting on auto pilot (albeit a changing auto pilot that takes account of what we learn) or making a genuinely free choice. I usually respond that the key questions to ask would be:

- Are we aware of what our normal pattern, and any current limitations, are telling us to think and do?
- Are we willing to act more powerfully than what our normal pattern, and any current limitations, are telling us to do?

If both answers are 'yes', then I call that 'making a free choice'.

In the next chapter I'll outline how AAT enables us to act powerfully, despite any current limitations.

Determinism in relationships

We've said we don't have to apply 'determinist thinking' to ourselves in the present, since if we're aware of an unhelpful pattern we can choose to change it. But 'determinist thinking' does always apply to the way others are thinking and behaving. As I've said, understanding that others are doing the only thing they could be doing, doesn't change their self-awareness. So 'determinist thinking' always applies to others in the present. This has big implications in the area of conflict and relationships.

Understanding the other person is saying or doing the only thing they could possibly be saying or doing (and has always said and done the only thing they could have said or done), can immediately impact the way we think about them and relate to them.

'Determinist thinking' eliminates blame and the 'should haves' in our thinking. But it doesn't eliminate judgement. We may still think the other person has said or done something unwise, selfish, inconsiderate or uncaring. Any of those judgements could be true. But we at least now know that's the only thing they could have said or done. We may still see some negatives in who the other person is, but we at least now know it's the only person they could have been right now.

Organisations

Paccepting other people's behaviour on the grounds they were doing the only thing they could have done, applies as much to organisations as it does to individuals. Organisations are, after all, made up of individuals, all of whom are doing the only thing they could be doing, all the time, given who they are at each moment.

The two justifications

We've outlined two justifications for Pacceptance (accepting what is):

1. It's too late to change what's already happened or 'what is'. AAT calls this the 'time-based' justification.

2. 'What is' (including what was) couldn't possibly have been different. AAT calls this the 'determinist' justification.

The time-based justification is initially easier to understand and use, which is why I introduced it first in this book. Nevertheless I often bypass it in therapy and introduce 'determinist thinking' first. The determinist justification is significantly more powerful as a means of generating self-acceptance and countering regret, self-blame, guilt, low self-esteem, blaming others and relationship issues. It's also more powerful in providing a basis for change. Where helpful, the two justifications can be used together.

3.

Accepting Feelings; Choosing Actions

Accepting uncomfortable feelings is one of the most powerful psychological tools available today. It's a key aspect of a number of acceptance-based therapies including Rational Emotive Behaviour Therapy (REBT), Acceptance and Commitment Therapy (ACT), and Mindfulness. CBT has been relatively slow to recognise the importance of this tool, but is now catching up with the developments of 'third wave CBT'.

There are two almost universally unhelpful human traits. The first is that most people go through life 'resisting' uncomfortable feelings. As I explained in Chapter 1, resistance in AAT means 'having negative thoughts about something' or 'wanting something to be different'.

The second unhelpful trait arises from the first. We tend to allow uncomfortable feelings to drive our behaviour. We'll come to this later.

The first trait is unhelpful for two reasons. First, resisting uncomfortable feelings generally makes them worse and / or sustains them. There's an expression that applies to many things in life, but particularly to uncomfortable feelings .... 'what we resist will persist'.

Resisting anxiety can lead to feeling anxious about feeling anxious. For example, the main driver of anxiety speaking to groups, by far the most common anxiety, experienced by most people at some time in their lives, is being anxious about feeling anxious.

In AAT, a significant part of the cure for anxiety is to stop resisting the anxiety, to be willing to feel anxious for now. In the case of anxiety speaking to groups for example, this is supported by understanding we can feel anxious and still speak.

A more extreme example is panic attacks. These are almost always a result of feeling anxious about feeling anxious. The more anxious we feel, the more anxious we get about feeling anxious and so anxiety escalates in a vicious cycle. In AAT, the prime cure for panic attacks is to be willing to feel anxious and, if necessary, to be willing to experience a panic attack.

Resisting depression can similarly make us depressed about feeling depressed. In AAT, a significant part of the cure for depression is to accept what we're feeling for now.

Resisting any other feeling will also generally make the feeling worse. Resisting feeling cold will generally make us feel colder. Resisting a craving will generally make the craving worse.

Impact on behaviour

The second reason that it's unhelpful to resist uncomfortable feelings is that resistance can lead to, or encourage, what I've already described as the second unhelpful human trait ….. our tendency to allow uncomfortable feelings to drive our behaviour. If we feel anxious, we tend to avoid whatever is making us anxious. If we feel depressed we tend to withdraw or isolate. If we feel angry we tend to retaliate. If we have a craving we tend to consume whatever we're craving. In most of these examples (all except anger), not wanting to feel what we're feeling will be a significant part of what's driving our behaviour.

So far, this is consistent with the behavioural principles of CBT. But AAT takes the view that the prime reason these behaviours are unhelpful is that they reinforce unconscious beliefs driving the feeling. (CBT generally only recognises conscious thoughts and beliefs).

Let's take the example of a client with a dog phobia.

All feelings are driven by a belief. The dog phobia is clearly driven by a belief, mainly an unconscious belief, that dogs are threatening or dangerous. The reason I say 'mainly unconscious' is because, at a conscious level, our subject has plenty of evidence that dogs are not generally dangerous. He can see everyone else walking past dogs, or playing with dogs, and not getting bitten.

He may well be confused as to why he has his phobic reaction to dogs, while faced with so much evidence that dogs are generally safe. Unknown to him, the explanation is that his negative belief about dogs is primarily unconscious. And our unconscious takes little notice of evidence or rational thinking. As we'll see, it primarily takes notice of our behaviour.

Our subject is walking along the pavement and sees a dog approaching. This triggers his unconscious belief, which in turn generates a fearful thought. The fearful thought triggers a release of adrenaline which races round his body generating anxiety. His heart is beating faster. His breathing accentuates. He may have a dry mouth and throat. He may be experiencing spasms. He may be trembling. And he may be perspiring.

He'll probably now do what he's always done to deal with his fear and anxiety. He'll cross the road to avoid the dog. He knows this will make him safe. And he knows from experience it will make him feel better. Now here's the key question that, in AAT, drives so much of human psychology. When he's crossing the road, what's happening to his unconscious belief that's driving his phobia? It's being reinforced. As he crosses the road, the message picked up by his unconscious, which thinks in fairly simple ways, is "If I'm crossing the road to avoid the dog, the dog must be dangerous".

I could ask my client if he knows why he has his phobia. He might say "Yes, I was bitten by a dog when I was young and ever since then I've been frightened of dogs". And I'll say "that's not the reason at all; that was just the trigger for your initial avoidance behaviour. You have your phobia for one reason and one reason only. For many years you've been avoiding dogs and every time you've done that you've reinforced the unconscious belief driving your phobia".

From an AAT persepctive, this reinforcement process is universal. Every time we do what a feeling (or a belief, or even a thought if it's driven by an unconscious belief) is telling us to do, we reinforce the unconscious programming or beliefs driving that feeling or thought.

- Every time we avoid something that's generating anxiety we reinforce the unconscious beliefs driving the anxiety
- Every time we withdraw and isolate due to depression we reinforce the unconscious beliefs driving the depression (life isn't good; I'm no good; the future isn't good, etc)
- If we have an 'anger problem' (getting angry a lot about small things), then every time we respond angrily, we reinforce the unconscious belief (about injustice) that's driving the anger
- Every time we consume something we're craving, we reinforce the unconscious belief that's driving the craving (which is that we 'need' whatever we're craving)
- Every time we carry out an OCD behaviour, we reinforce the unconscious belief that's driving our compulsion, and that's driving the anxiety we then experience if we don't carry out that behaviour

The cure

The prime 'cure' for all these issues is already understood from the behavioural tools of CBT. We need to repeatedly do the opposite of what the feeling is telling us to do. We need to stop crossing roads and walk past the dog. For depression, we need to stop withdrawing and engage with life. For cravings or addictions, we need to stop consuming whatever we're craving. For OCD, we need to cease the OCD behaviour.

But there are two important differences between AAT and CBT in this regard.

First, CBT suggests we need to reverse the behaviour primarily to change conscious beliefs. CBT argues that each time we walk past the dog (hopefully without being bitten), the experience is teaching us that dogs are safe. To reinforce this learning CBT might even add a cognitive exercise, such as a Thought Record, to focus our conscious mind on evidence that dogs are safe.

The problem with all of this is that our phobic client already knows at a conscious level that dogs are safe. He's presented with evidence of this every day as he sees others walking past dogs.

By contrast AAT focuses on unconscious beliefs and how these are either reinforced or challenged through our behaviour. In practice we've found that this focus on unconscious beliefs gives clients a much clearer understanding of a) how they inadvertently created their problem, b) how they've been constantly reinforcing it, c) why their problem has continued to grow despite any rational conscious reasoning telling them that it doesn't seem justified and d) they now know they have a clear choice between continuing to reinforce their problem or taking action to unwind it.

If doing what a thought or feeling is telling us to do reinforces the unconscious beliefs driving the thought or feeling, then doing the opposite will undermine those beliefs. My phobia client needs to stop avoiding dogs and start walking past them. Each time he does this, he'll challenge and undermine the unconscious belief driving his phobia. The message picked up by his unconscious is then: "If I'm walking past the dog, it must be safe." Repetition of the behaviour will undermine, and eventually remove, the unconscious belief driving the phobia. If he wants to accelerate his cure, he can stop and pat the dog. If he wants to cure his phobia in a week, he can buy a dog.

The second difference between AAT and CBT approaches is that AAT places a much greater emphasis on dealing with feelings.

When I tell my phobia client that to cure his phobia he needs to stop avoiding dogs and walk past them, he's already feeling pretty anxious just listening to me. When he's facing his first dog, his anxiety will be sky high. To help him to deal with that anxiety I need to convince him that it's OK to feel anxious. I need to train him to accept his anxiety.

There's hardly any issue that's brought to me as a therapist where 'accepting feelings' is not a key aspect of AAT treatment.

Accepting feelings

In AAT there are two aspects of accepting uncomfortable feelings. The first is a willingness to fully experience the feeling. This is counter intuitive to most clients as, in the absence of advice to the contrary, most people spend their lives trying to avoid or diminish uncomfortable feelings.

The second aspect is being able to say to ourselves, with some conviction, that it's OK to be feeling whatever I'm feeling, as long as I'm feeling it.

I explain to clients that when we talk about accepting feelings, it doesn't mean it's OK to be feeling the same way five months, five days or even five minutes from now. After all, the purpose of coming to therapy is more often than not, a desire to diminish uncomfortable feelings. It just means it's OK to be feeling this way for now. It's OK to be feeling whatever we're feeling as long as we're feeling it.

The first thing I do is to provide two bits of information about feelings:

1. First, feelings are harmless. No-one has ever been harmed by a feeling. Anxiety, depression, anger, desires, cravings and compulsions are all totally harmless. We may be harmed by what we do as a result of a feeling. People sometimes harm themselves when feeling depressed. But the feeling itself is harmless.

    Even feeling cold is harmless. We may be harmed by the source of a feeling. The source of feeling cold is being cold. Being cold can kill us. But 'feeling' cold is just a messaging system that lets our brain know that our body is cold and we need to do something about it. 'Feeling' cold is harmless. The same applies to eating too little food versus 'feeling' hungry.

Prolonged or repeated feelings such as stress can have long-term medical consequences but, at the time, feeling stressed for now (which is usually primarily about feeling anxious) is harmless.

2. Second, feelings are bearable. The only feeling that's unbearable is extreme pain, probably under torture. With that level of pain we cease to be able to function. Lesser feelings don't have that consequence and so we say they're 'bearable'. My dog phobia client might try to dispute this. He might suggest that I don't know how unbearable his anxiety becomes when he's near a dog. I'll ask him to describe his anxiety. He might say his heart is racing, his breathing is going crazy and he's sweating like a pig. I'll ask him if he's ever run for a bus. Assuming he says 'yes', I'll ask him what was happening to his heart rate and breathing and whether he was perspiring, when he reached the bus. Then I'll ask him if he could bear it.

I suggest my clients ask three questions about any uncomfortable feeling they may experience. The questions are designed to move them away from resistance and towards acceptance, of the feeling. I emphasise the questions are about the feeling itself, not the source of the feeling. The '3 questions', together with suggested answers, are:

1. Is this feeling harming me?	No! No-one has ever been harmed by a feeling
2. Can I bear it?	Yes! Anything less than extreme pain is bearable
3. If it's not harming me, and I can bear it, what exactly is the problem with having this feeling for now, other than that it's uncomfortable	It's OK to have the feeling, for now, and for however long I'm feeling it

The shower exercise

To help my clients train themselves to accept uncomfortable feelings, I suggest they try this exercise. Next time we're in the shower turn down the hot water a little …. just enough so we feel a bit uncomfortable. Run through the above '3 questions' and answers in our mind. Note the questions are about the uncomfortable feeling, not the cool water.

I may suggest a couple of added questions:

- Could I choose to stand here for another 10 seconds, despite the discomfort? Then do that.
- If I wanted to, or needed to, or was sufficiently motivated to (someone was offering me a large sum of money to do it), could I choose to turn off the hot water completely and stand here

for a minute? We don't have to do that. Having born the small discomfort for ten seconds, we can turn the hot water up again. The point is to understand we could have chosen to experience greater discomfort, and remain uncomfortable for longer, if we'd been sufficiently motivated to. That might be useful to know as, when my subject walks past his first dog, he'll be very anxious for about a minute. And he's clearly motivated, as he's come to see me to cure his phobia.

We've now experienced being able to accept discomfort and choose an action opposite to what the discomfort is telling us to do.

We can repeat the exercise, either straight away (if we found it easy enough) or on another occasion. When we're ready and willing to, we can further reduce the temperature and / or stand there feeling uncomfortable for longer. Keep increasing the challenge until we've handled discomfort that's as severe as, and perhaps for as long as, the discomfort we expect to experience when we 'walk past the dog' or whatever other behaviour we need to adopt to begin to unwind limiting unconscious beliefs.

We can now use the same '3 questions' to enable us to accept any uncomfortable feeling.

Other exercises

There are other exercises we can use to practice the 3 questions. Walking (or running) up several flights of stairs. Walking (or running) up escalators instead of standing. Taking any form of exercise while accepting muscle pain, heavy breathing, tiredness, etc.

The key learning from these exercises, and asking the 3 questions, is that it isn't just the discomfort that's driving unproductive behaviour. It's mainly the way we think about the discomfort.

The AAT approach of accepting uncomfortable feelings, is similar to Acceptance and Commitment Therapy (ACT), with the addition of the '3 questions' that lead us towards acceptance .... and using the shower and other exercises to practice those 3 questions.

In the follow-up session, if I judge they've understood and benefited from the shower exercise, I may supplement the learning by mentioning there's a bonus. They never need suffer from feeling cold again. They'll still feel cold, but they can just accept it and choose not to 'suffer' as a result of the feeling. The same can apply to any other feeling.

Accept the feeling; choose the action

So the key AAT cure for most mind-based issues is to repeatedly accept the feeling and do the opposite of whatever the feeling is telling us to do. In short: 'accept the feeling; choose the action'. The '3 questions' help us to accept the feeling. After sufficient practice, we can skip the first two questions and go straight to the third.

- For anxiety ... accept the fear or anxiety and choose not to avoid, or escape from, whatever is making us fearful or anxious

- For depression ... accept feeling depressed and choose to fully engage with life (and take exercise)
- For cravings or addictions ... accept the desire or craving and choose not to consume the substance
- For anger problems (excessive anger over minor perceived injustices), accept the anger and choose to withhold the response
- For OCD, accept any compulsion driving the OCD behaviour and choose to avoid the OCD behaviour (and accept any further anxiety that may result from avoiding the behaviour)

If we do this repeatedly, the unconscious programming that's driving the feeling or compulsion will unwind.

The AAT focus on accepting feelings has numerous benefits:

a) It builds a realisation that feelings are OK. This counters the assumption that most people have, that uncomfortable feelings are not OK and need to be avoided.

b) Accepting uncomfortable feelings always diminishes those feelings, whereas resisting them makes them worse.

c) Accepting uncomfortable feelings enables us to take powerful action despite whatever we may be feeling.

d) Accepting feelings, alongside the behavioural change, directly contributes to unwinding limiting unconscious beliefs.

A case example illustrates the last benefit.

Cathy suffered from a phobia of flying. She had received a promotion that required her to take periodic flights. She booked herself onto a 'fear of flying' course run by a major airline. The course was CBT-based. On the cognitive front they revealed statistics demonstrating the safety of flying. On the behavioural front, they then took participants on a flight and recommended they fly as much as possible. By the time Cathy came to see me, she'd flown perhaps six more times and was still terrified of flying.

Cathy had done everything the course required, but it wasn't working. I asked her to describe her typical flying experience. Predictably she'd begin to feel anxious in the days leading up to the flight. The anxiety would increase as the day approached. The night before she'd hardly sleep. The anxiety would continue to increase as she approached the airport and then the plane. She'd be in a state of near panic as she boarded the plane and would usually have her first panic attack as the plane accelerated down the runway. She'd periodically shake during the flight, sometimes spilling coffee and panic again in the event of turbulence and on approaching the landing.

She was aware of the cognitive input of the course, including the statistics showing that flying is safe. But the beliefs driving her anxiety were primarily unconscious, and our unconscious mind takes little notice of rational evidence.

Furthermore, the course had not addressed accepting her anxiety. In our first session I taught her all the tools we've covered around accepting feelings, including the '3 questions' and the shower and related exercises. By the time I saw Cathy again two weeks later she'd practiced the tools and flown again. She said the experience was very different and her anxiety had been contained. I saw her twice more during which she flew several more times. She was completely cured of her phobia.

Adding Pacceptance

Accepting feelings can be viewed as just another example of Pacceptance. Pacceptance after all is a combination of 'accepting what is' and, where feasible and desirable, taking action to improve the future. So 'accept the feeling, choose the action' is itself another Pacceptance tool.

But there are other ways that Pacceptance can be used to support this tool. If we're having resistant (negative) thoughts about our current issue, we can use Pacceptance by accepting what is (it's the only situation we could have been in right now) and choose to repeat the opposite action. If we're having resistant thoughts about our realisation that we've created our problem, through repeatedly acting in reinforcing ways, we can Paccept this (it's the only thing we could have done, given who we were at the time). If we're having resistant thoughts about the challenges of the cure, we can Paccept this (using the AAT worry tools).

Letting Go of Uncomfortable Feelings

Once we've fully accepted uncomfortable feelings, we can often let them go.

Accepting uncomfortable feelings disempowers those feelings, usually diminishes them and stops us resisting them and so reinforcing them.

But despite accepting our feelings and choosing opposite actions and so unwinding our unconscious limiting beliefs, some residual feelings can sometimes remain because the unconscious beliefs that are driving them have become conditioned or habitual.

When this is the case, we can often 'let go' of those residual feelings.

Letting feelings go isn't always an option. It depends on the individual and the issue. The following are some criteria which generally influence the likelihood of success.

- The feeling should have been fully accepted for a while
- The feeling should have diminished already as a result of using acceptance and 'accept the feeling, choose the action'

- The feeling should now be mild to moderate, not severe
- The client should be reasonably functional and rational, as indicated by an ability to understand AAT tools and apply them

Letting go of uncomfortable feelings isn't the same as suppressing them. Suppressing a feeling takes focused effort and is nearly always unhelpful. Letting go of a feeling is just a choice, based on a decision that we don't need the feeling any more.

Trying to let a feeling go before we've fully accepted it is generally just another form of resistance and is unlikely to succeed. If it does succeed, it's likely we're suppressing the feeling and it will return.

I've been able to help clients let go of mild depression, anxiety, anger, irritation, guilt and embarrassment, once those feelings have been fully accepted.

Acceptance is still the most important attribute and letting go of feelings should never be at the expense of accepting them.

4.

Relationship Challenges

Challenges in relationships is a common issue arising in therapy, whether in individual therapy or, more commonly, in couples or family therapy.

In individual therapy, issues might involve relatives, partners, friends, work colleagues, business associates, organisations or others. In couples therapy it's more likely to primarily involve partners. In all these cases AAT offers a number of tools that help us to handle relationship challenges.

Owning our Reactions

If I have a fear of mice then, when I see a mouse, I'll experience a programmed reaction, driven by an unconscious belief that mice are somehow threatening. I'll then project my reaction onto the mouse, and so view the mouse as somehow frightening and the cause of my reaction.

But when we're reacting to something or someone, our reaction is happening in our own minds, and is based on our own unconscious beliefs that drive our automatic ways of thinking and feeling.

What we're reacting to is just the trigger for our programming. The trigger isn't the cause of our reaction. The cause is our own beliefs (primarily unconscious) and our own unconscious reactive programming. If we're able to recognise this, our reaction is likely to rapidly diminish. I call this 'owning our reaction'.

Owning our reaction enables us to separate the reaction from the trigger and view them separately. It gives us an understanding of what's really going on.

If at the same time we can accept any feelings that might be involved in our reaction, it's likely to diminish further.

Our reactions are made up of automatic thoughts and feelings. (Any resulting behaviour we call a 'response'). As our reaction is automatic, we have little immediate control over those thoughts and feelings. We are, however, able to choose our actions or behaviour (our response).

You'll recall from the previous chapter, that if we allow our reaction to drive our behaviour, we'll reinforce the unconscious beliefs driving the reaction. If I want to unwind my reaction to mice, we already know I need to accept the feeling and choose the (opposite) action; i.e. don't jump up on a chair if that's what I'm thinking of doing and, even better, visit a pet shop and hold a mouse.

Owning our reactions is a powerful tool for dealing with challenges in relationships. If someone has said or done something, or is saying or doing something right now, that I don't like and I'm reacting with feelings of irritation or annoyance, owning (and accepting) my reaction will diminish it, and make it easier to Paccept what's happening.

Withholding any negative response will avoid reinforcing my reaction programming and start to unwind it, if that's what I want to do.

'Determinist thinking'

The second AAT relationship tool is determinist thinking. As you already know, this is a powerful basis for Paccepting someone else's behaviour. What they've just said or done is unquestionably the only thing they could possibly have said or done, given who they are right now.

'Determinist thinking' removes blame and diminishes irritation, frustration and other reactions. It negates any thoughts that others could and should have behaved differently or should be behaving differently right now.

Perspective

The third AAT relationship tool is about 'perspective', the collection of internal processes that drive our thoughts and behaviour at any moment. It's worth knowing that we all think we're right and reasonable all the time. The problem is the other person also believes this. Indeed we **are** always right and reasonable 'from our perspective'. And so is everyone else, no matter what they might be thinking, saying or doing.

An argument or disagreement is about each person trying to persuade the other to adopt their perspective. This rarely succeeds unless it's about facts and we can prove we're right and they're wrong. Most disagreements are about opinions and we can rarely change another person's opinion through argument.

What is far more effective is to try to understand the other person's perspective and then look for compromise or win-win solutions.

If you and your partner want to see a different movie. You could argue about the merits of each movie, but it should be clear that neither is uniquely right or wrong. Clearly you're both right from your perspective. A win-win solution might be to see your movie today and his or her movie next week. Compromise solutions might be to find a third movie you both like, or to forget about the movie and go out to dinner.

Taking responsibility

The fourth AAT relationship tool is 'taking responsibility for other people's behaviour'. This may initially sound strange as clearly everyone is responsible for their own behaviour. But 'being responsible' is slightly different from 'taking responsibility'.

'Determinist thinking' says that others are doing the only thing they could be doing, given who they are right now. We're all on auto pilot practically all of the time, driven by who we are at each moment and our perspective at that moment.

Usually the only way we can change our way of thinking or our perspective is as a result of external input. As you read this book, hopefully some of your ways of thinking are changing. If so, you're a slightly different person than you were before you started reading this book.

So if we're having a challenging or conflictual exchange with another person, each of us is only likely to change our thinking as a result of the input or influence of the other person. Hence it makes sense to take responsibility for the other person's behaviour. They can't change right now without our input.

We've said that if we become aware of an unproductive pattern that's driving our behaviour we can change it. But how likely is it that the other person will have that insight right now? In practice the only person who's in a position to do something to break their pattern is us. We might be able to achieve this by doing something out of the norm, such as stop arguing, suggest a compromise, tell them they have a point, suggest perhaps we're both right (from each of our perspectives), compliment them for something they've done or are doing right, or anything else that causes them to stop and think in a different way.

Combining the tools

We now have four AAT tools that can be used individually or together to help us deal with any challenge in relating to others.

In my experience the best way to practice these tools is to use them in a sequence, find out what works best for us, then select those we prefer in any given situation. My recommended order is:

- **Own (and accept) our reaction.** Recognise it's about us. The other person is just the trigger for our programming. This will immediately diminish our reaction.
- **'Determinist thinking'.** Understand the other person has said or done (and is still saying or doing) the only thing they could have said or done. This will further diminish our reaction.
- **Perspective.** Understand the other person believes they're right and reasonable, just as we do. This will again diminish our reaction. Try to understand the other person's perspective. We can then consider a compromise or win-win solution.
- **Taking responsibility.** The other person is saying or doing the only thing they could be saying or doing, given who they are right now. The only person who's in a position to change their thinking or their perspective is us. We may need to say or do something different from our norm, or different from whatever we've already tried.

I-statements

Another useful relationships tool, not developed as part of AAT and even pre-dating CBT, is the I-statement. This is a polite way of asking someone to change their behaviour without criticising them. When we criticise others it's likely they will try to defend, or even counter-attack.

An I-statement lets the other person know how we're feeling, takes responsibility for that and asks them to help us to manage our feelings, usually by changing their behaviour.

A typical I-statement might be along the lines of:

> "When you do what you do, I feel upset. I know that's my problem, not yours, but it would really help me to deal with my problem if you could stop doing what you're doing."

Do I-statements always work? No. Two possible reasons:

- The other person isn't interested, despite your request
- They may see it as a manipulation to try to get them to change, which to be perfectly honest, it usually is

Forgiveness and Reconciliation

Owning our reaction, understanding others were, and are, doing the only thing they could be doing, considering perspective and taking responsibility for the other person's behaviour, are all tools that can help us to Paccept others and their behaviour.

Pacceptance in turn can lead to forgiveness. For me and most others I've trained, Pacceptance is enough. If we're Paccepting someone who we believe has done us wrong, there may be little to forgive.

Where we've fallen out with others, anger and blame towards the other person can be accompanied by regret, guilt or self-blame for the part we've played in the falling out.

We may need to first Paccept ourselves and our behaviour and then Paccept others involved (we and they have always done the only thing we could have done).

In helping my clients deal with guilt and resentment, I usually find that Pacceptance is sufficient. Taking this on to the extra step of forgiveness, however, is sometimes helpful. For more religious clients, forgiveness is often something the client sees as important. It is also sometimes helpful when the client wishes to reconcile with a past adversary.

Reconciliation can be a powerful tool for clients who are living with resentment and a sense of injustice. It's usually only helpful or necessary when the client has fallen out with someone who is still significant in their lives. Sometimes there may be a practical motivation for reconciliation, such as reconciling with a previous partner for the benefit of shared children.

An AAT approach to reconciliation might involve:

- Understanding that both of us were doing the only thing we could have done, given who we were at the time
- Sharing how each feels and felt in a non-blaming way, perhaps using I-statements
- Each apologising for their part

It might help if both have read this book.

Reconciliation is often fearful, so the client may need to first accept their own feelings, using the '3 questions'.

5.

Owning and Choosing Our Experience

The concept of 'owning our reactions' can be extended, by the same logic, to owning our entire experience .... of everything. Things happen, but our experience of those events or situations happens in our own mind. And the nature of that experience depends on our own attitudes, beliefs and ways of thinking.

Just as 'owning our reaction' is about recognising that our reactions are all about us, so 'owning our experience' is about recognising that the way we experience an event or situation is about us too.

As with our reactions, we tend to project our experience onto the event or situation that triggered it and blame the event or situation for our experience, without acknowledging or even realising that the way we experience things is about us.

This idea isn't new. William Shakespeare was aware of it when he had Hamlet say (in Act 4) "There's nothing good or bad, only thinking makes it so".

AAT's contribution to an idea already expounded by Shakespeare, is twofold:

- First, AAT attempts to highlight the significance of Shakespeare's wisdom, both in our lives and in the context of therapy. We can only imagine how many people have seen Hamlet, acknowledged Shakespeare's eloquence and left the play without even realising its significance and, quite probably, never giving it another thought.
- Second, Shakespeare may have understood the significance of what he expressed through Hamlet, but there's little evidence that he knew much about how to change our experience. That's a key aim of AAT.

Regarding the second point, CBT provides some tools for changing the way we experience events and situations, primarily:

- Changing our cognitions by understanding 'cognitive distortions' and identifying evidence for and against negative thoughts
- Changing behaviour to challenge our cognitions and beliefs
- Tools, such as 'Thought Records' and 'activity records' to further the above aims

AAT provides different tools:

- Pacceptance using two logics:
  a) The 'time-based' rationale of accepting the past and present (it's too late to change them) and future ('whatever will be, will be')
  b) 'Determinist thinking'
     o Understanding that the past and present are the only thing they could have been, but the future is wide open
     o Accepting ourselves (as, right now, we're always the only person we could have been)
     o Understanding that taking responsibility for our past actions is primarily about changing future behaviour
     o Understanding that we can only exercise genuine "free will" in the present moment by being aware of our limiting patterns and acting powerfully to change those patterns, while accepting any uncomfortable feelings this might generate
- For major worries, supplementing 'whatever will be will be' with recognising exaggerations of probability and/or consequence.
- Accepting feelings (using the '3 questions' and exercises to practice those questions)
- 'Accept the feeling; choose the action' (adding 'accepting feelings' to CBT's behavioural tools and an understanding of either reinforcing

    or unwinding unconscious beliefs and programming)
- Relationship tools:
  - o Owning (and accepting) our reactions
  - o Understanding that others are saying and doing the only thing they could be saying and doing
  - o Considering other people's perspective
  - o Taking responsibility for other people's behaviour
- Owning our experience

6.

The Therapy Process

That Extraordinary Truth

The 'determinist' principle, which is that we've always done the only thing we could have done, given who we were at the time, is one of the most widely used principles in AAT. It also may initially seem, to some, the most radical.

I mentioned in Chapter 2 that when I began using it in therapy, I assumed that, because it seems so radical, it would be resisted by many of my clients. I was surprised to discover this wasn't the case. On the contrary, I find the vast majority immediately understand it, acknowledge the truth of it and find it hugely helpful.

There has been the odd exception. A couple of my clients, out of thousands, either couldn't fully understand it, or couldn't accept it as being true, or maintained a view that there might be something negative about using it, even if it were true. When I couldn't easily persuade them otherwise, I've simply dropped it and moved on to other tools.

Before introducing the idea, I normally preface it by saying "I'm going to tell you something that may at first seem strange because it's very different from the way we've all learned to think".

It usually takes no more than 10 to 20 minutes to convince a client of this truth. Sometimes they need to think about it between sessions and I'll answer any questions when they return.

It's advisable not to get bogged down in any discussion of the extent to which the future is truly 'open'. I usually suggest we leave this to the philosophers, while we take advantage of the benefits of understanding that the past and present could not have been different.

Once the client has grasped it, 'determinist thinking' can immediately change the way they think about the issue they've brought to therapy. Any regret, guilt and self-blame immediately fall away. Other changes occur when we apply 'determinist thinking' to others.

Most clients come to therapy with, to some degree, diminished self-esteem. They may feel guilty or ashamed for having their problem. They may think they're weak for having their problem. Or they may think that in some other way the existence of their problem makes them a lesser person.

Understanding that there's no way they could have avoided their problem, may not remove such issues entirely. They may still not like who they are right now. But for most clients it removes any sense of self-blame, which is generally a significant component of diminished self-esteem.

If the issue brought to therapy is specifically about self-esteem, then combining the AAT approach of 'determinist thinking' with the CBT approach of examining strengths and weaknesses and focusing on the positives, can provide a broader approach to dealing with the issue.

When clients come to therapy they're generally seeking a number of outcomes: dealing with the past, self-acceptance, acceptance from others, resolution of their problem and hope for the future. Understanding that the past and present could not have been different, is a major contribution to meeting the first two needs. Understanding that we, the therapist, know this as well, is a contribution to meeting the third need. Understanding that a change in awareness is all that's needed to change the future is a significant contribution to meeting the final two needs. They may not have expressed it to themselves in these terms, but coming to therapy is a powerful step they've already taken to change how they think and behave.

One example of clients who benefit immediately from understanding they've always done the only thing they could have done, given who they were at the time, are those carrying guilt or shame about something they've done. We'll see other examples when we look at specific cases.

While most clients take fairly easily to the idea that they've always done the only thing they could have done, applying this to others is often more challenging. If others have hurt us or let us down, it's often hard to acknowledge those people were doing the only thing they could have done. If it applies to us, it must also apply to others. But while this makes sense, it may be emotionally more challenging to adopt this line of thinking. Hurt, anger, resentment, bitterness and blame cannot always be easily brushed aside by rational thinking.

Sometimes it's a case of planting the seed and waiting for it to grow. Accepting feelings, and owning our reactions, are also helpful in enabling a client to think more rationally.

It's also important to remember that even if something is true, we have a choice as to whether we take account of that truth in our thinking. It may be true that others were doing the only thing they could have done, but if they've been cruel or knowingly or intentionally unfair to others, we can always choose not to apply the truth of 'determinist thinking', if we don't wish to. It's our choice.

But intentional cruelty is rare. Most people believe their actions, even if selfish, are somehow justified. If it seems relevant, I may explain this to a client and then revisit the question of whether the other person was really being intentionally cruel or knowingly unfair.

When the client's issue involves anger, resentment or blame, understanding that the other person was doing the only thing they could have done, will invariably help in resolving that issue.

Another example of an effective application of 'determinist thinking' is depressed clients who present a history of challenging life experiences. Their history may be focused on the pain they've experienced as a result of the actions of others or on their own perceived failings.

As well as empathising with their experience, I find it universally helpful for them to learn that everything that's happened in their lives so far is the only thing that could possibly have happened, given who everyone was at each moment.

I've experienced a number of clients where this understanding has quickly resolved even severe depression. In most cases other AAT tools such as 'accept the feeling; choose the action' will also be needed.

With depressed clients, I'll usually start with accepting feelings and 'determinist thinking'. With anxious clients, I'll usually start, as in CBT, with psycho-education about what anxiety is, then move on to the AAT tools of accepting feelings and 'accept the feeling; choose the action'.

Accepting what is

Either before or after (usually after) persuading my clients that they and others have always done the only thing they could have done, given who they were at the time, I'll usually introduce them to the broader concept of 'accepting what is' and 'accepting what will be'.

I personally used to be a prolific worrier. I completely eliminated worry from my life in a few weeks by repeatedly replacing worry with 'whatever will be will be' and using this tool until it became my natural way of thinking.

I've already mentioned that I chose to get tough with myself. I refused to allow myself to maintain a resistant thought on the grounds that all resistant thoughts are irrational. I personally prefer the term 'crazy', i.e. all resistant thoughts are crazy, as I found it motivated me more to get rid of them. We perhaps have to be more careful about using that term with therapy clients.

I recommend my clients follow the same approach. Most succeed in quickly eliminating resistance of the past, present and future, from their lives.

Pacceptance

It's a small jump to move from 'accepting what is' to Pacceptance, which simply adds refocusing on any action we can and want to take to improve the future.

While I initially introduce Pacceptance in the context of 'accepting what is' (which includes accepting what was), I later explain that Pacceptance includes accepting what will be …. the prime antidote for worry. I explain that worry is also irrational (wanting the future to be different from the way we think it might be, in an area that we believe we cannot control). And I'll mention Doris Day's song 'Que sera sera; whatever will be will be' and the 'mother and daughter' story that it tells.

If, in a subsequent session, 'accepting what will be' proves insufficient to rid my client of worry, I'll provide further tools, including the tool about exaggerating probability and / or consequences and understanding that, with practice, we'll be able to Paccept whatever happens.

Accept the feeling; choose the action

For most clients, either before or after introducing the concepts of resistance versus   Pacceptance and determinist thinking, I'll tell them the story of the dog phobia, leading to an understanding of reinforcing versus unwinding unconscious beliefs and introducing the tool 'accept the feeling, choose the action'

I'll explain that accepting feelings is powerful in four ways:

a) It builds a realisation that feelings are OK. This counters the assumption that most people have, that uncomfortable feelings are not OK and need to be avoided.

b) Accepting uncomfortable feelings always diminishes those feelings, whereas resisting them will make them worse.

c) It enables us to take powerful action despite whatever we may be feeling.

d) Alongside the behavioural change, it directly contributes to unwinding limiting unconscious beliefs.

Relationship tools

I regularly provide my clients with the four AAT tools that I introduced in the chapter on relationships. The four tools can, with practice, be used in the sequence that I described towards the end of that chapter.

Forgiveness and Reconciliation

Understanding others were and are doing the only thing they could have done, owning our reactions, taking responsibility for, and choosing, our experience and taking some responsibility for the other person's behaviour, are all tools that can help us to Paccept other people and their behaviour.

Pacceptance in turn can lead to forgiveness. For most, Pacceptance is enough. If we're Paccepting someone who we believe has done us wrong, there may be little left to forgive.

In some cases where clients have fallen out with others, anger and blame towards the other person can be accompanied by regret, guilt or self-blame for the part the client played in the falling out.

The client may need to first Paccept themselves and again, this can lead to forgiving themselves if this is what they need to do.

In helping my clients deal with guilt and resentment, I usually find that Pacceptance is enough. Taking this on to the extra step of forgiveness, however, is sometimes helpful. For more religious clients, forgiveness is often something the client sees as important. It is also often helpful when the client wishes to reconcile with a past adversary.

Reconciliation is a powerful tool for clients who are living with resentment and a sense of injustice. It usually only arises where the client has fallen out with someone who is still significant in their lives. Sometimes there may be a practical motivation for reconciliation, such as reconciling with their previous partner for the benefit of shared children.

Reconciliation is often fearful, so the client may need to first accept their feelings.

Paccepting it all and opening up the future

When the client has grasped the concept of Pacceptance and has been successfully using it for a while, I usually introduce them to the idea of 'Paccepting it all'. If we've all been doing the only thing we could have done, given who were at the time, how could any aspect of the past, or any situation that exists right now, have been different. So we have every reason to Paccept it all.

Whatever the client's issue, whatever their circumstances, whatever has happened in the past, none of it could have been different, given who everyone was at the time.

But the future is wide open. A change in our thinking and behaviour is all that's needed to set us off on a new path. A combination of Pacceptance and use of the 'accept the feeling, choose the action' can create the change that's needed.

If the client has been limiting themselves in some way in the past, it's because they didn't have the awareness of how to break through those limitations. Increasing our awareness gives us more choice, or at least enables us to make more powerful choices.

As the client begins to take more responsibility for their future, the possibilities expand.

Understanding this is often all the client needs to break through long-held issues, beliefs and limitations. When the lights come on, clients can rapidly make major changes in their attitudes, behaviour, mood and their lives.

This is of course the aim of all therapy. But AAT provides the opportunity to address the concept of self-awareness more directly.

Comparisons with other therapies

AAT is a cognitive and behavioural therapy. However, like other cognitive and behavioural therapies such as Rational Emotive Behaviour Therapy (REBT) and Acceptance and Commitment Therapy (ACT), AAT is not CBT.

Given the dual acceptance and action focus, AAT may sound similar to ACT. In fact it's very different. The prime similarity is that both therapies advocate accepting uncomfortable feelings. Beyond that there are few similarities.

ACT encourages acceptance of negative thoughts as well as feelings. By contrast AAT, like CBT, encourages us to challenge negative thoughts, though, like CBT and ACT, it does advocate accepting negative thoughts where challenging them proves difficult for the time being. Particular examples of the latter might be worry and obsessive thoughts (such as beliefs that we may not be able to stop ourselves harming ourselves or others).

A major difference between AAT and CBT is that AAT focuses on 'accepting what is' as a prime mechanism for challenging negative thoughts. In AAT, 'resisting what is', in other words wishing the past or present were different, is viewed as the major thought distortion, whereas CBT focuses on a range of thought distortions such as exaggeration, black and white thinking, emotional thinking and focusing on negatives.

CBT uses the Thought Record as a primary mechanism for challenging thought distortions. AAT uses 'Pacceptance' as a prime tool.

AAT probably has more similarities to Rational Emotive Behaviour Therapy (REBT) than to CBT or ACT. While REBT doesn't specifically focus on 'accepting what is', it does challenge our tendency to want every situation to meet our expectations or preferences. This is also a prime focus of AAT, though the mechanisms are different, with REBT focusing on challenging 'musts' and 'shoulds' while AAT focuses directly on 'accepting what is' and 'accepting what will be'. A further similarity is REBT's principles of self-acceptance and tolerance of others, features closely shared by AAT, though again using different mechanisms, with AAT focusing on determinist thinking.

Alone or combined?

AAT can be used effectively on its own, but I wouldn't expect this to always be the case. Just as REBT, ACT and Mindfulness can be used in conjunction with CBT or other therapies, the same is true of AAT.

When CBT was born, initially as Cognitive Therapy, it was developed as a cognitive treatment for depression. It has since expanded, absorbing behavioural therapy and developing new approaches for just about every emotional and behavioural disorder.

The same could happen with AAT or any of the other newer therapies such as ACT, but this seems unlikely.

Since CBT is now so extensive, it makes sense to use it alongside the newer therapies where appropriate, rather than expanding the newer therapies to cover all of the same ground.

Hence AAT is not put forward as a universal therapy. It is proposed as a powerful therapy that can be applied alone or in conjunction with other therapies where appropriate.

My own therapy practice is roughly 80% AAT, 15% CBT and 5% other approaches, such as Rewind for post-traumatic stress disorder (PTSD), Time Line Therapy and occasional use of hypnotherapy.

****

The following chapters explore the application of AAT in treating various common issues, using case examples. I've tried to avoid repeating details provided in earlier chapters, so you may wish to make reference to these. Names and some details have been changed to maintain anonymity.

7.

Depression

Robin had been depressed on and off for much of his life. It had started at school and continued through college and for the following 18 years to the time I met him.

He was an only child and had felt unloved and unsupported by his parents. He'd been sent to boarding school from a young age and felt his parents had never really wanted him. He sensed they were more interested in their own careers and their own lives and he felt he'd been a burden to them.

In the school holidays he'd often been sent to stay with relatives on the excuse that his parents needed to travel.

He'd become depressed in his final two years at school. This affected his academic performance and so he was unable to attend the college his parents had wished for him. He'd wanted to please them and thought he'd failed them.

At college he'd drifted in and out of depression. He saw a counsellor which helped for a while, but the depression soon returned.

He left college before completing any qualification. He wasn't sure what he wanted to do and moved from job to job, looking for something he could enjoy. He still spent much of his time depressed, often triggered by the realisation that his latest job was proving to be no more satisfying than the last one.

He'd experienced some psychodynamic therapy but it hadn't helped. He hadn't tried medication as he was concerned about potential side effects. A friend had endured a bad experience with anti-depressants.

The few relationships he'd started had been short-lived, so in his late thirties he was still single. He felt life was passing him by.

Session 1:

When I met Robin he was going through a low phase and was clearly depressed. Our first session involved hearing his story but I'm keen that wherever possible my clients leave the first session with something to do.

I explained to him the value of accepting feelings, describing our tendency to 'resist' uncomfortable feelings, thereby reinforcing, or at least maintaining, them. I described how 'resistance' can result in us becoming anxious about feeling anxious or depressed about feeling depressed. I mentioned the adage 'what we resist will persist'

I described the '3 questions' (see the table in Chapter 3) as a tool to aid accepting feelings, explaining that feelings are always both harmless and bearable.

He was willing to experiment with 'accepting feelings'. I gave him the shower exercise (see below the table in Chapter 3). He agreed to give it a try. I suggested that whatever he got out of this exercise he should try applying it to his depressed feelings.

I suggested he focus on his feelings a few times a day, fully experiencing and accepting them. I suggested that when he asked himself the '3 questions', end by saying to himself, with as much conviction as he could muster, "it's OK to be experiencing this feeling for now".

Finally I explained the benefits of taking exercise to counter his depression and how he could use 'accepting feelings' again using the '3 questions', to deal with any discomfort he may experience while exercising. He agreed to put this into practice.

Session 2:

When I saw Robin a week later, he said the shower exercise had given him an insight into a different way of thinking about his feelings. He'd applied it to his feeling of depression as I'd asked him to. He said he felt better each time he did so. While the feeling had increased again in between, he thought overall his depression had diminished over the week.

He'd started taking exercise and had used the 'accepting feelings' approach to deal with discomfort that arose.

I mentioned that many find that a bonus of the shower exercise is that they never need suffer from feeling cold again. They'll still feel cold, but they can accept that feeling and not suffer as a result. The same can apply to accepting any other feeling.

I asked him what he believed to be the key thought behind his depression. He said that while originally it had been about the lack of caring from his parents, he believed now it was about having wasted his life.

I asked him whether he blamed himself for his perceived 'missed opportunities'. He said he did. He particularly felt his decision to leave college prematurely had been a mistake that had adversely effected the rest of his life.

Having warned him I was going to tell him something he might initially find strange, I explained that when he decided to leave college that was the only thing he could possibly have done. He said he thought he could and should have chosen a different action.

I then explained 'determinist thinking', the fact that we've all always done the only thing we could have done, given who we were at the time and the fact that who we are at any moment is always the product of our life history up to that moment. (See Chapter 2).

While Robin had never heard this before, he saw the truth of it straight away. He quickly understood that all the choices he'd made were the only choices he could have made, given who he was at the time.

He also quickly understood that everyone else who'd influenced his life in any way had also been doing the only thing they could have done, and hence that who he was right now was the only person he could possibly have been.

I explained that he was still responsible for his past actions but this responsibility was only relevant to the actions he took now and in the future. He acknowledged that with a change of awareness and a consequent change in thinking and behaviour, he could become someone different.

I suggested he spend some time during the week thinking through his regrets and the actions that had triggered those regrets and acknowledge that in each case he did the only thing he could possibly have done. I suggested he then apply the same thinking to things that others have done.

I also suggested he apply that thinking to day to day events as they occurred. He agreed to continue to accept his feelings and take exercise.

Session 3:

Robin said he could now see that both he and others had always done the only thing they could have done, at every moment of his life. He said he no longer blamed himself or others for everything that had happened.

He said that letting go of self-blame and blaming others had been a great help and his depression had further diminished.

He also understood that who he was right now was the only person he could possibly have been right now.

I reinforced the understanding that while the past and present were the only outcomes they could have been, the future was wide open. He confirmed he was willing to do whatever was necessary to create the future he wanted.

We then turned to the concept of 'accept the feeling; choose the action'. I explained how most people tend to go through life allowing their feelings to determine their actions. I explained how every time we do this we reinforce the unconscious beliefs driving the feeling.

I used the example of a dog phobia, described earlier in this book. He quickly understood that accepting feelings and taking the opposite action unwinds the unconscious beliefs driving our recurring feelings.

We discussed the extent to which allowing feelings to drive behaviour was the case in Robin's life. He conceded that when he was depressed he tended to withdraw, stay at home and not make any effort to move his life forward.

He could now see how this was reinforcing his depression and that the more productive approach would be to 'accept the feeling and choose the opposite action'.

We made a list of some things he could do, in addition to exercise, that would counter his tendency to withdraw. At my suggestion it included developing a passionate interest (for him that was photography), doing some voluntary work and thinking about how he could contribute more to his employer beyond carrying out his normal role.

[Note this step is similar to behavioural activation in CBT for depression. The difference with AAT is the emphasis on accepting feelings in combination with taking action and the understanding that we always have a choice between continuing to reinforce, or to unwind, our unconscious beliefs].

Session 4:

The next time I saw Robin, his mood had again lifted. He even seemed excited about possibilities for the future. He'd begun using the adage 'accept the feeling; choose the action' and had started taking action in several areas on his list.

We talked about what he wanted to do with his future, covering career, relationships and interests. We talked about what would need to happen for these to come to fruition and what actions he might need to take.

I introduced him to some of the power tools covered in my 'Positive Mind Training', a webinar-based development training. We spent some time setting goals, including taking steps to increase his chances of finding a relationship. For each goal we identified which of the power tools were relevant and how they could be applied.

[Note: with most therapy clients, it would not be appropriate to cover power tools at this stage, which are more about coaching than therapy. Robin was particularly keen to get into action and take control of his future, so in his case it seemed timely].

Session 5:

Robin had started taking action on his goals.

We now turned to his parents. Robin thought they'd been uncaring in their attitude towards him. He now understood they'd always done the only thing they could have done, given some apparently (to Robin) uncaring attitudes they may have had. Robin wanted to know if they could have avoided developing, or maintaining, those attitudes?

We talked this through until Robin understood we could never have avoided our past. Everything that's happened in our lives has been determined by who we and others were at each moment. We can only ever change the future by becoming aware of attitudes or patterns that aren't working for us or for others and choosing to change them. That applied to Robin's attitudes to his parents as much as everyone else.

We explored whether his parents really were uncaring and developed a more balanced view. We established that Robin's mother had appeared to be the more caring but had been influenced by the more disciplinary attitude of his father. We recognised his father's attitudes had been formed by his own life history in his childhood, his school and later in life.

Robin said he was confident he could let go of blaming his parents for the past but still found his past disappointing. He also found it disappointing that he'd only just learned about the determined nature of life and said it would have been useful if he'd known about it earlier … though he acknowledged that, in a determined world, this simply couldn't have happened.

I told him that just because something was unavoidable doesn't necessarily make it agreeable. We can still be disappointed by the past or present if they don't meet our preferences about how they might otherwise have been.

I introduced him to the concept of 'accepting what is' and the technique of Positive Acceptance (Pacceptance). I pointed out the two justifications for 'accepting what is': the 'determinist' justification we'd already discussed and the 'time-based' justification …. the fact that it never makes sense to wish the past or present were different as it's too late to change either. I explained the latter approach can be useful when we're still disappointed despite acknowledging that the past and present could not have been different.

I explained we still have the choice to drop any regrets and disappointments and focus on how we can improve the future. I encouraged him to start using Pacceptance on minor issues as they arose day to day and then apply this way of thinking to any disappointments. (He'd already dealt with his regrets, self-blame and blaming others, using 'determinist thinking').

Session 6

Robin had practiced Pacceptance every day (using both justifications for 'accepting what is') and found it to be powerful. He said it gave him a sense, for the first time, of being in control of his thoughts and hence his mood and feelings.

We talked more about his relationship with his parents. He was seeing them every few weeks but said the relationship had always seemed superficial.

I introduced him to the principles of 'owning our reactions', taking responsibility for our experience, choosing our experience using all the tools we'd already discussed and 'taking responsibility for both sides of any interaction', the latter being based on our understanding that the other person is doing the only thing they could be doing, given who they are right now, unless we intervene.

We talked about what he might say to his parents if he had an honest conversation with them. We talked about letting them know how he'd felt, about his feelings now, about how he'd realised they'd all (he and them) been doing the only things they could have done.

The prospect of this conversation was fearful for him but he was willing to 'accept the feeling; choose the action'. Nevertheless he was more comfortable having the conversation just with his mother initially.

Session 7

When I next saw Robin, he was no longer depressed. He'd practiced the various tools we'd introduced in the previous session.

He'd had the conversation with his mother and felt it had gone well. He'd used some of the tools during that conversation. He hadn't yet had a chance to talk to his father but was now keen to do so.

We spoke about the Pacceptance principle of 'Paccepting it all'. We spoke about possibilities for the future and recapped the various principles and tools he'd learned and used during our time together. This was our last session and Robin left confident that he now had the tools needed to avoid becoming depressed again.

8.

Anxiety

Mark had first experienced significant anxiety when he was studying for his final school exams. He realised too late that he'd spent insufficient time on his studies. He became anxious leading up to the exams. He believed anxiety experienced during the exam had further affected his performance.

Anxiety continued to affect him through university. He had some counselling but the problem remained and developed further. He continued to experience exam-related anxiety, developed social anxiety and experienced significant anxiety whenever he needed to present in class, even if he was just participating in a class discussion.

He believed he hadn't got the job he desired as a result of anxiety experienced in interviews. He finally obtained a job and now, six months later, was still suffering from presentation anxiety. He was getting anxious in meetings and in one-to-one discussions with his boss and senior management.

Mark had tried CBT-based counselling but it had focused on 'Thought Records', an evidence-based approach to challenging his fears, generally of little value in dealing with anxiety, and behavioural approaches, of much greater value, but without being accompanied by accepting feelings, proved to be too challenging for Mark to implement.

Session 1

After hearing Mark's story, I initially followed the standard CBT approach of educating him on what anxiety is (an adrenaline-based fight-flight response to fearful thoughts).

I explained that 'resisting' feelings tends to make them worse. In the case of anxiety, we can become anxious about feeling anxious which just makes us more anxious. I mentioned the adage 'what we resit will persist'.

I asked him what he thought the opposite of resistance might be. I explained the benefits of learning to 'accept' uncomfortable feelings. (It stops us resisting them and so usually diminishes them and sometimes causes them to disappear).

I introduced him to the AAT principle and techniques of accepting uncomfortable feelings (see Chapter 3).

I described the '3 questions' to ask about any uncomfortable feeling (will it harm me? can I bear it? so what's the problem with having the feeling?).

I gave him the shower exercise (see Chapter 3 following the table). I suggested that whatever he got from the shower exercise, he applied to his feelings of anxiety, and any other uncomfortable feelings.

Session 2

Mark had been practicing accepting his anxious feelings, using the '3 questions', and confirmed this had diminished the feelings. He'd carried out the shower exercise and said it had helped.

I mentioned that many people find that a bonus of the shower exercise is that they never need suffer from feeling cold again. They'll still feel cold, but they can just accept it and not suffer as a result. The same can apply to accepting any other feeling.

He also said the psycho-education had helped as he was no longer afraid of his anxiety symptoms.

We turned to the CBT approach of identifying avoidance. Mark was clearly avoiding events that could generate social anxiety and opportunities that might generate anxiety speaking to individuals or groups.

I explained how this avoidance was reinforcing the unconscious beliefs driving his anxiety and why reversing the avoidance would have the opposite effect. I used the example of the dog phobia (see Chapter 3).

I introduced the AAT tool 'accept the feeling; choose the action', explaining that to resolve a problem involving uncomfortable feelings we need to repeatedly accept the feeling and choose an action opposite to whatever the feeling is encouraging us to do. In the case of anxiety, we need to accept the anxiety and do whatever is making us anxious.

Mark was clearly encouraged by this understanding. He said it was scary but he was thankful he now had an approach that made sense and provided the promise of a way out … and hope for the future.

He agreed to seek opportunities to socialise with friends and attend social functions.

I recommended he join Toastmasters, a public speaking club that provides a safe place to speak in front of groups, deal with speaking anxiety, gain public speaking abilities and, through this, generally enhance confidence.

He committed to practice accepting any anxious feelings while he took on these challenges.

Session 3

Mark was making progress. He'd joined Toastmasters and had already spoken in front of the group, which he described as frightening but encouraging. He'd stopped avoiding social and work-based opportunities and was continuing to accept his anxiety.

He said the adage 'accept the feeling; choose the action' was a mainstay of his new approach and was giving him confidence to face his fears.

On hearing his story, it became clear Mark considered he'd brought his problem on himself by not leaving enough time to study for his final school exams. He also thought he should have been able to deal with his anxiety symptoms more effectively and so prevent the problem escalating to its current level.

We were able to alleviate these self-effacing views through the determinist principles of AAT (see Chapter 2 …. we've always done the only thing we could have done, given who we were at the time). While he'd not come across this thinking before, he understood and accepted it straight away.

I suggested he spend some time during the week considering any other regrets and self-blaming thoughts he may have about his life and use 'determinist thinking' to eliminate them.

Session 4

Mark had resolved his regrets about the part he played in how his anxiety had initiated and developed. He said he'd also let go of other regrets using 'determinist thinking'.

We could have ended the therapy there and Mark would have continued to make progress under his own steam. However, in my experience, learning and applying all aspects of AAT is a confidence booster for anyone and so a big help in dealing effectively with anxiety. I gave Mark that option and he elected to take it. We covered the remaining AAT skills in the balance of this session and three further sessions:

Current session:	Accepting ourselves and extending the determinist principle to others
Session 5:	Pacceptance and stop worrying
Session 6:	The AAT relationship tools and taking responsibility for our experience
Session 7:	The power tools covered in my 'Positive Mind Training' web-based development training

Mark's confidence continued to grow as he applied these skills and by the final session his problems were fully resolved.

9.

Self Esteem

Becky was suffering from low self-esteem. She was in her late 20s when I met her. Her life thus far had been challenging.

Her father had been violent, physically abusing her mother, her younger brother and herself. Despite the abuse, she had formed an attachment to her father before he left. She never saw him again, learning later that he died some years after leaving the family.

Becky had become withdrawn after her father left. She had put on weight and been bullied at school. Having performed poorly academically, she dropped out of school at 16.

She had left home, got involved with drugs and drifted between unemployment and jobs which seldom lasted long, usually due to her poor reliability.

Her relationships had been similarly transient and short-lived.

She had received counselling which had helped her to a degree but had not significantly impacted her approach to life or her low self-esteem. She had received funding to see me for up to four sessions.

Session 1

The first session primarily involved Becky telling her story. It quickly became apparent that her low opinion of herself and her consequent low self-esteem and poor prospects were her central issues. It was also clear that she largely blamed herself, and in part her father, for her experience of life to date and her seemingly poor prospects.

In view of the time constraints, some progress needed to be made in the first session.

Without my usual warning of "I'm going to tell you something that may surprise you", I simply told her as though it was an obvious truth that everything she'd ever done in her life was the only thing she could possibly have done at each moment and that who she was now was the only person she could possibly have been right now.

She was clearly surprised.

We had time for little more than these basic explanations:

- Everything we do in response to our circumstances is determined by who we are at the time .... our ways of thinking, our attitudes, beliefs, abilities, knowledge, unconscious programming and so on.
- Who we are at any moment is the product of all our experiences up to that moment, including all our thoughts and the choices we're made along the way. And all those choices that have determined who we are right now, were also the only choices we could

have made given who we were at each moment.

- We're still responsible for our past actions, but this responsibility is only relevant to what we do now and in the future.

She left to think about what I'd told her.

Session 2

I'm constantly amazed at the ability of clients to absorb and process information that's radically different from the way they've always thought. It's not universal, but it's certainly the norm.

Becky was not the most educated client I've ever helped. But she was bright and adaptable. When I saw her a week later she'd worked out the significance of what I'd told her. She'd already let go of blaming herself for her past failings.

She understood that who she was now was the only person she could have been. But she'd also worked out for herself that the future didn't have to be like the past … that what she does in the future depends on her choices in the future and that 'who she is now' could change.

She'd even worked out that if she'd always done the only thing she could have done, then so had everyone else, including her father.

She was willing to acknowledge that he was still responsible for his actions even though they couldn't have been different. She imagined that somehow his death might have been a reflection of that responsibility.

I explained to Becky that letting go of blaming

herself and her father was a strong basis for accepting her past and who she is right now. All that was now needed was some tools to take control of the future.

We began by teaching her how to accept her feelings. She periodically experienced feelings of depression, anxiety and anger. All of these could be dealt with through acceptance. I gave her the shower exercise (see below the table in Chapter 3).

We covered the benefits of accepting feelings including the prime benefit of being able to separate our feelings from our actions. I gave her the adage 'accept the feeling; choose the action'. We made a list of actions she could take that were opposite to those suggested by her feelings and that could move her life forward. These included:

- Turning up to work on time whatever she was feeling, providing she wasn't ill
- Doing what her supervisor wanted, irrespective of her current feelings about her job
- Commencing an exercise programme that she would keep to
- Commencing a diet that she would follow, irrespective of any desire she may have to eat more than, or less healthily than, the diet permitted. She elected to join Abicord's weight management programme.

Becky understood that she needed to accept her uncomfortable feelings, and unproductive desires, all the time, while she followed the actions she'd agreed to.

Session 3

Becky had carried out all the activities we'd agreed. She was genuinely excited about the possibilities for a different future. She'd taken in a lot of information in the previous session and I needed to clarify that accepting feelings involved being willing to experience them fully and not trying to avoid or suppress them.

She also needed some psycho-education on the nature of anxiety and re-assurance that anxiety symptoms are harmless and bearable and could be resolved through total acceptance of the feeling and choosing to do whatever was making her anxious.

Her activity programme had taken on a momentum of its own. She had even told her supervisor that she was going to approach her work and her life differently without any suggestion from me to do so.

Also without any suggestion from me, she'd watched my development training webinar. And finally, without any suggestion from me, she'd dressed more smartly for this our third session.

We used this session to teach her about 'accepting what is' and the technique of Positive Acceptance (Pacceptance). She already knew about 'determinist thinking', so it wasn't a big step for her to understand the alternative time-based justification and to put these two justifications into the wider context of Pacceptance.

Session 4

Becky had been using Pacceptance throughout the week. As with all who learn and use it, she found it to be powerful. She said that for the first time she sensed she was in control of her life.

She had already lost some weight and was feeling healthier following just two weeks of her weight management programme.

Her esteem had clearly increased significantly. Most importantly, she was hopeful about the future. We recapped what we'd covered:

- We and others have always done the only thing we could have done, at each moment, given who we were at the time
- Who we are right now is the only person we could have been right now, but our future is wide open
- Accepting uncomfortable feelings and 'accept the feeling; choose the action'
- Pacceptance

I asked Becky about her aspirations for the future. She felt the most important near-term goal for her was achieving her weight target. She felt this was significant to gaining confidence and achieving the relationship she desired. She also wanted to find work in the fashion industry.

We spent the balance of her final session going through the power tools outlined in my web-based development training. We used her weight loss and career goals to illustrate use of these tools.

Becky left with the confidence she would achieve her goals. I felt she would too.

10.

OCD

Paula had suffered with Obsessive Compulsive Disorder (OCD) for well over 10 years. It had begun at school and expanded during her time at university. She had not been able to keep a long term relationship and was now concerned she probably never would unless she did something about her issue.

Her OCD was contamination-based. Her behaviour included washing her hands many times a day. She tried to avoid touching anything that others may have touched, such as door handles or money. If she did, she'd have to immediately wash her hands. She discarded the first section of toothpaste every time she squeezed the tube. She had a particular fear of batteries, scanning the pavement for possible discarded batteries whenever she was out walking.

Paula had been in counselling several times. Sometimes this had helped, but had not resolved her problem. The most successful treatment to date had been CBT. This had included cognitive work to challenge her conscious beliefs about contamination and behavioural work to encourage her to cease her OCD actions. It had included 'positive exposure', intentionally exposing her to perceived contamination by touching things that others had touched without washing her hands.

The CBT treatment had reduced Paula's OCD behaviour, but it had subsequently returned.

AAT treatment:

The key differences between AAT and CBT in the treatment of OCD are:

- 'accepting what is' …. primarily using 'determinist thinking', to remove regret, guilt and self-blame in relation to the client's history and current condition
- Recognition that the beliefs driving mental health issues reside primarily in the unconscious, whereas CBT focuses on conscious thoughts. The unconscious mind takes little notice of rational thinking or evidence, one of the key focuses of CBT
- Recognising that the client has unwittingly created her OCD problem by repeatedly reinforcing her unconscious beliefs through OCD behaviour
- Using acceptance to control the compulsions driving OCD behaviour and the anxiety resulting from stopping the behaviour
- Using the '3 questions' to facilitate acceptance of compulsions and anxiety
- Using the shower and other related exercises to create discomfort and so practice accepting feelings.

- Combining acceptance of compulsions and anxiety with the CBT tool of withholding OCD behaviour

Session 1

After hearing Paula's story, I introduced 'determinist thinking' and explained the above-mentioned benefits

Session 2

I introduced Paula to the concept of 'accept the feeling; choose the action', using the dog phobia as an illustration (see chapter 3). She now understood how her issue had developed, how she had continually reinforced and sustained it and what she needed to do to resolve it.

I gave her the 3 questions and the shower and related exercises, to practice accepting feelings. I explained how she needed to use these tools to accept her compulsions …. and the anxiety which results from not responding to them.

Session 3 (some weeks later)

We used this, our final session to recap the tools and review how she was doing in applying them. She had ceased all her OCD behaviour. The behaviour has not re-commenced after several years. If the treatment had not been so successful, I would have considered use of 'positive exposure' in line with her previous CBT treatment. For most AAT treatments of OCD, this has not proved necessary.

11.

Obsessive Thoughts

Obsessive thoughts are highly negative thoughts driven by irrational beliefs.

One type of obsessive thought is the belief that we'll harm ourselves or others without being able to stop ourselves. Typical obsessive thoughts of this type include believing we'll uncontrollably jump in front of a car or train or off a balcony, that we'll harm our children, that we'll drive off the road or into on-coming traffic or that we'll uncontrollably stand up in an audience and shout or scream. These thoughts are always imagined as they're never realised.

Another type of obsessive thought is based on superstitious beliefs.

Alex was an example of the second type. As a result of reading something, she became concerned about the number '2'. She began avoiding writing that number, believing that if she did, something negative would happen in her life. This soon expanded to avoiding speaking the number. Her belief that something negative would happen grew to believing that a disaster would happen in her life.

These avoidances spread to anything connected to the number 2. She would avoid anything involving pairs. When I met her, she was wearing two different socks.

For some time before I met her, she hadn't been able to do anything twice. She couldn't take the same route twice, eat the same meal twice or wear the same combination of clothes twice.

She had sought help from a number of therapists without success. One had told her the problem lay in her childhood and had spent a number of sessions exploring her childhood. Another had told her she had a problem with the wiring in her brain. A psychiatrist had told her she needed drugs. An unscrupulous therapist even told her she'd probably been sexually abused as a child.

The only therapy that had helped was CBT. The CBT therapist had identified evidence from her experiences that challenged her superstitious beliefs and had tried to get her to reduce her avoidant behaviour. The cognitive challenges had little impact on her unconscious beliefs (the unconscious takes little notice of rational evidence) but nevertheless helped her to implement the behavioural changes. Those behavioural changes had an impact for a while but weren't sustained.

Session

Once I'd heard her story, I told Alex I would explain both how she'd created her problem and how she could resolve it. I told her I'd do this by reference to an unrelated mental health issue, so she could understand the principles involved without the distraction of thinking about her own problem.

I related the dog phobia example (see Chapter 3). Alex was both surprised and intrigued. She now understood how she'd unwittingly created her own problem and how her behaviour was continuing to reinforce and sustain it.

I asked her how she'd cure the dog phobia. She was able to work this out herself (see Chapter 3). She now understood why the CBT therapist had tried to get her to reduce her avoidance behaviour and she now understood, how that would unwind the unconscious beliefs driving her problem, something the CBT therapist probably didn't know and so hadn't explained. But from her own experience, she recognised that the dog phobia client would experience high anxiety when he tried to walk past the dog.

I explained the role of accepting feelings and the shower and other related exercises. I summarised that the key AAT tools used to resolve almost all mind-based problems were contained in the adage 'accept the feeling; choose the action'. I also told her that in the case of 'obsessive thoughts' if she found it difficult to rationally negate the thought right now, in her case the superstitious thought, then she should accept that too for now, using the same '3 questions'.

Alex now had everything she needed to resolve her problem. I didn't need to see her again. I heard from her two weeks later. She'd completed all the exercises within a few days and since then stopped all her avoidant behaviour. She contacted me again another few weeks later. Her issue was completely resolved.

12.

Anger

Michael was another survivor of a broken marriage. When his father left he was 12 years old. He coped by becoming more assertive. He got into fights at school and became more difficult to control.

He had maintained contact with his father but the relationship remained difficult and conflictual.

His anger problem continued through his early adult years. He lost jobs as a result of his tendency to generate conflict. He was referred to me by an employer who valued his work enough to want to keep him.

Session 1

While Michael was aware he had a problem, he was also quick to blame others for the conflicts that had led to disappointments in his life.

Two of his job losses he blamed on 'incompetent' bosses. He spoke extensively of the inadequacies of others and portrayed his problem as 'not suffering fools gladly'.

[Most AAT work commences with either accepting feelings or introducing the determinist principle to deal with self-blame and blaming others. Blaming others is a key aspect of anger problems so the determinist principle is generally a good place to start, but it's important to always introduce the concept in relation to blaming ourselves as this is the easier aspect to understand and acknowledge].

I asked Michael whether he had any regrets. He said he regretted an argument he'd had with his father before his father left home. He had for a long time blamed himself for his father leaving.

I asked him whether he thought he could have handled that argument differently. He recounted that he'd said some cruel things that it would have been better not to have said. Perhaps his father might then not have left.

I asked what he might think if I were to suggest he couldn't have avoided saying those things. He said he was aware of what he was saying, so he could have chosen not to say them. But he was angry and chose to say things he knew to be hurtful.

I said I had to disagree with him. I said that even though he was aware of what he was saying, in my view he couldn't have chosen not to say what he said. Something making up 'who he was' would have had to be different. Something about his way of thinking. Or something about the way he made choices in challenging situations. In short, something about Michael would have had to be different.

And that wasn't possible. At the moment he chose to say the things he said, Michael was who he was. He would have needed to be someone slightly different at that moment in order to have said something different.

I went on to explain that we've all always done the only thing we could have done, given who we were at the time. I explained how 'who we are' comes to be what it is at any moment as a result of all our life experiences up to that moment. And I explained the difference between blame and responsibility (see Chapter 2).

Finally I explained that who he was right now was the only person he could possibly have been right now, but that the future could be very different with a change of awareness.

Michael understood and said he'd never looked at things that way before. I suggested he spend some time thinking about it during the week and try applying this way of thinking to any other regrets, guilt or self-blame he could think of.

Session 2

Michael had indeed thought about 'determinist thinking' during the week. He said it had made a big difference. He said it might have been helpful if this had been taught in school, so he wouldn't have had to spend all those years thinking he could, and should, have avoided the break-up of his family.

I suggested that even if he couldn't have behaved differently in his argument with his father, it seemed unlikely his father would have left home just because of an argument with one of his children. Michael agreed that it might have been more complex.

In response to his earlier point, I said I hoped it would be taught in schools one day but the knowledge, understanding or awareness to do so simply wasn't there when he was at school.

I used the opportunity to point out that what applies to us applies to others too. His teachers, school administrators and the education policy makers had also always done the only thing they could have done.

He said he supposed the same was true of his father. I said it certainly was. There was no way his father could have not left home. I said that in order for him to have made a different choice he'd have needed to have been a different person. And the only way he could have been a different person was if something in his history up to the time he made that choice had been different ... and that was never possible.

We discussed other examples, both in relation to his father and in relation to others at work and elsewhere who Michael had been in conflict with from time to time.

I suggested he spent time during the week thinking about past instances in his life when he'd blamed others or thought they 'should' have acted differently, and reconsider them in the light of what we'd said.

Session 3

Michael had not only done what I asked, he had, without my prompting, started to use the determinist principle in dealing with day-to-day issues. He had a difference of opinion with someone at work and had realised the other person had been doing and saying the only thing he could have been doing and saying, given who he was at the time.

Michael said this realisation had come later, not at the time. At the time he'd felt annoyed and frustrated.

I confirmed that it's difficult to engage in rational thinking such as 'determinist thinking', when we're feeling emotional.

I explained the technique and benefits of accepting uncomfortable feelings such as anger or frustration. I explained an immediate benefit is that in order to accept a feeling such as anger, we need to focus on the feeling which takes our attention away from whatever or whoever triggered it, so diminishing the feeling. In fact accepting frustration or anger, or any other feeling, always diminishes the feeling.

I told him that the bigger long-term benefit of accepting uncomfortable feelings is that it allows us to separate our feelings from our actions. It enables us to 'accept the feeling; choose the action'.

I briefly outlined the story of the dog phobia (see chapter 3). I explained that in order to resolve a recurring feeling that's causing a problem in our lives, the action we choose should always be the opposite of the action suggested by the feeling. In the case of a problem with anger or frustration, we need to accept the feeling and choose not to respond in an aggressive way,

I explained that if we were able to do this consistently for a period of time, the unconscious beliefs that drive the feelings, such as beliefs around injustice laid down in his childhood, would unwind.

I explained that, by contrast, if we always respond to an angry feeling with an aggressive response, then the unconscious beliefs that drive the angry feelings will be reinforced (since our unconscious receives a message that the belief driving the anger must be justified).

[This was a lot for Michael to take in. I sometimes separate learnings around accepting feelings and 'accept the feeling; choose the action' over two sessions. But I considered Michael was able to handle it all in one session].

I gave him the shower exercise (see after the table in Chapter 3) to try at home and left him to practice accepting his feelings and using the adage 'accept the feeling; choose the action'.

Session 4

Michael had again carried out the exercises we'd agreed. He confirmed that focusing on and accepting his feelings of frustration and irritation had immediately diminished them.   And he confirmed that he'd consistently held back on any angry responses. He'd again been tested at work in an interchange with someone he regularly disagreed with. He said he'd simply focused on and accepted his feelings. He said it gave him a sense of being able to choose his response rather than simply being driven by what he was feeling.

We used this fourth session to introduce him to the concept of 'accepting what is' and the technique of Positive Acceptance (Pacceptance). I explained the two justifications for Pacceptance .... the 'determinist' justification, which he was already familiar with, and the 'time-based' justification (it never makes sense to wish things were already different).

We also recapped what we'd covered previously:

- Dealing with regret and resentment using the determinist idea that we and others have always done the only thing we could have done
- Accepting feelings and using the adage 'accept the feeling; choose the action'.

I suggested Michael try using Pacceptance every day whenever he found himself wishing something were different (always the case whenever we're dissatisfied about anything), or whenever he found himself thinking he or someone else shouldn't have said or done something they'd said or done.

I reminded him that using the Pacceptance tool sometimes had to wait until uncomfortable feelings had subsided but that accepting those feelings would speed up this process.

Session 5

Michael had found Pacceptance to be powerful. He said he now felt he had a great deal of control over the thoughts that drove his feelings and that used to get him into trouble. He said he noticed he was feeling angry less often and even when he did feel angry he was able to accept the feeling and hold back any response. He was then able to Paccept the situation by understanding the other person had said or done the only thing they could have said or done, given who they were at the time.

I introduced Michael to the concept of owning our reactions. I told him this would further enhance his ability to accept his feelings, hold back on any angry response and Paccept whoever or whatever had triggered his reaction.

We talked about taking responsibility for our experience which occurs naturally when we own our reactions.

We talked about perspective and trying to see issues from the other person's perspective.

And finally we talked about taking responsibility for both sides of an interaction, including the other person's behaviour, based on our understanding that the other person is doing or saying the only thing they could possibly be doing or saying right now, given who they are at the time, unless we intervene.

He took these ideas away to practice during the week.

Session 6

Michael had integrated the new learnings into his day-to-day life. His anger problem was resolved, so this final session proved to be an opportunity to recap and to give him some more tools covered in my webinar-based Positive Mind Training.

13.

Addiction and Guilt

Simon came to me for treatment of a gambling addiction. It quickly became clear his problem was being exacerbated by a high level of guilt around the damage his addiction had already done to his family.

He had lost all his family's savings, the family home and a substantial inheritance his wife had received from her parents. In addition he was in significant debt.

He was still employed and was earning a reasonable income that in the absence of his addiction would be sufficient to support his family and service his debt.

His wife had only recently discovered his addiction and the extent of the losses and had told him she would leave him if he didn't stop gambling. That was several weeks prior to him coming to see me. He had told her he had stopped. But he hadn't. He told me he didn't know how to stop and didn't know whether he could. He was sure his wife would find out and would leave him.

Session 1

Having heard Simon's story, I shared with him the determinist principle of AAT, saying that everything that had happened up to this moment was the only thing that could possibly have happened. He was surprised but understood and accepted it straight away.

I explained the difference between blame and responsibility. I suggested he now had every justification to let go of regret, guilt and self-blame, those thoughts all being invalid in a determined world, but that he still needed to take responsibility for his past actions. I explained that taking responsibility would only impact the choices he needed to make now and in the future. It would need to entail making amends to his wife and family for the impact he'd already had on them.

I asked him whether he was willing to resolve his addiction immediately. I suggested we extend the session to two hours. I assured him I would give him all the tools needed to break his addiction. He agreed. In fact the session lasted two and a half hours.

I introduced him to the adage 'accept the feeling; choose the action', using the example of the dog phobia. He now understood how he had created, reinforced and sustained his addiction and what he needed to do to unwind it. He said he was prepared to do whatever it took.

I gave him the shower and related exercises to generate discomfort and practice the '3 questions' (see the table in Chapter 3). I told him he'd need to apply acceptance, with the help of the 3 questions, to his desire and compulsion to gamble and to the anxiety he'd be likely to experience when he denied himself the opportunity to do so.

I also told him that for him to achieve an immediate and sustained cessation, he needed to make a commitment (an unbreakable promise) never to gamble again. I asked him to make the commitment to himself and to me in the session and later to his wife, his children and anyone else he believed would support him.

He was initially reluctant, on the basis that he would let so many others down if he broke the commitment. I agreed and told him that was precisely why he needed to make the commitment and share it with others. I gave him some other reasons why he couldn't even consider breaking a commitment. He'd be breaking an unbreakable promise, so challenging his integrity; his best chance of a cure would fail; he'd never come across a more effective cure and would probably remain a gambler for life and, finally, he would have thrown away a tool he could have used to achieve many other goals in his lifetime. He made the commitment.

I introduced two additional power tools taught in my web-based development training … 'acting as if' and 'focusing on contribution'. We also covered some other tools included in my smoking cessation treatment …. changing trigger points, time-line therapy and a brief session of hypnotherapy.

Session 2

We had one follow-up session to recap and reinforce the material covered in the first session. No further treatment was needed. This was several years ago. To my knowledge, Simon has never gambled again. His marriage was sustained and his debts have been repaid.

14.

Relationships

Steve and Laura had arrived at a turning point in their marriage. They'd entered marriage with high hopes and aspirations for the future based on what seemed to be a strong and caring relationship.

But this had been based on an unspoken and naïve assumption, held by each of them, that in time they'd be able to change those aspects of the other that didn't fit their ideal model of the perfect partner. In time those unaccepted characteristics had instead accentuated and begun to irritate.

They'd ironically been married for seven years when they came to see me. They had two children aged five and three.

Sessions 1/2

[I always see couples individually for the first session, giving them a chance to express their perspective without restraint from their partner's presence].

Laura's prime complaint was that Steve was devoted to his work and was unwilling to share in household and family duties. Steve's prime complaint was that Laura was controlling and constantly complained about his activities and perceived 'failings'.

[In those first sessions I also asked them what they believed their partner's prime complaints might be. Steve got it right. Laura thought Steve's complaint would be that she spent too much time with the children].

I asked them to each prepare three lists before we met jointly:

1. 3 positive things about the other person
2. 3 positive things about their relationship
3. 3 issues in the relationship they wanted to resolve in order of significance

[I don't ask for exhaustive lists as perceived omissions from the partner's first two lists can be a source of further upset and conflict].

Session 3

I began the first joint session by talking briefly about the fact that we all have different perspectives, that we all believe we're right and reasonable and the fact that we always are right and reasonable …. from our perspective.

I then asked them to share their two positive lists after pointing out that even these may highlight different perspectives.

Steve and Laura seemed happy with each other's positive lists and no particular issues arose.

I asked them how they thought we might best proceed to resolve issues on their third lists. After discussion, with some suggestions from me, we agreed that on raising an issue we would:

- avoid criticising by using 'I-statements' to raise the issue (see Chapter 12)
- describe what we believe to be the other person's perspective, with the other person then confirming or clarifying that assessment
- try to find compromise or win-win solutions that go some way to satisfying both party's needs

Each raised an issue and compromise solutions were reached following these guidelines.

I used the balance of this first joint session to introduce them to the determinist principle of AAT (see Chapter 2). I asked them if either had a regret they were willing to share. Steve offered his decision to study engineering rather than architecture. I was able to convince them that this was the only decision he could possibly have made given who he was at the time.

I then explained the difference between blame and responsibility (see Chapter 2).

While surprised, they were both comfortable with these ideas and could see the relevance to their relationship. I suggested they spend some time thinking about any regrets from a determinist perspective and keep the principle in mind when they considered the past and present actions of others, including each other.

Session 4

We commenced with a conversation about the determinist principle. I suggested we initially discuss it without reference to their relationship.

They both shared information on regrets and irritations in dealing with others such as parents, work colleagues, bosses and even a utility company (if individuals have always done the only thing they could have done, then so have organisations. They are, after all, only made up of individuals, all of whom have been doing the only thing they could have done all the time).

I asked them whether they thought it might be helpful to apply this thinking to their relationship. They agreed it would. We discussed how we might do this. It was agreed that the past was the only thing it could have been and all that mattered now was the future.

We added another guideline to the list developed in the previous session. When raising an issue we would:

- acknowledge that whatever had been said or done in the past, we were all doing the only thing we could have said or done at the time

Each raised a further issue and a compromise solution was reached using the guidelines developed so far.

I used the balance of the session to introduce them to the concept of 'accepting what is' and the AAT technique of Positive Acceptance (Pacceptance). They were already familiar with the determinist justification, so I only needed to familiarise them with the alternative 'time-based' justification (it makes no sense to wish things were already different).

I suggested they practice Pacceptance and apply it to day-to-day issues both within and outside their relationship.

They also agreed they'd work through the third issue on each of their lists at home.

Session 5

Both Steve and Laura had been using Pacceptance extensively and had found it to be powerful.

Steve gave an example at work when a printer had not delivered on time. He said he would previously have become irritated by the poor service and stressed by the knock-on consequences to his own service delivery.

He said he'd Paccepted the late delivery on the basis that it was the only thing that could have happened. As the printer was normally reliable, Steve hadn't felt he needed to take action for this one-time failing. The printer had in any event apologised.

Regarding the consequences to his own service delivery, following late delivery by the printer, Steve said he'd noticed himself becoming stressed and then realised he was wishing something was already different, dropped the negative thought and refocused on whether there was anything he could do to improve the situation. He said he'd contacted his customer and cleared the delay with them.

Laura gave an example of using Pacceptance when Steve arrived home later than expected. She realised it was the only thing that could have happened **and** that she was wishing something were already different. She said she'd dropped the negative thought and waited for Steve's explanation which, she said, turned out to be reasonable. They'd agreed he would call in similar situations in future.

Both said potential conflicts were now being avoided, the agreed new behaviours were being followed and communications had improved.

They told me about the issues they'd worked through at home and about the solutions they'd developed.

I used the balance of the session to introduce the AAT tool of accepting feelings. I explained the benefits including being able to separate our feelings from our actions and introduced the adage 'accept the feeling; choose the action' as a means of avoiding conflict.

I gave them the shower exercise (see Chapter 3 following the table) to try at home and suggested they practice accepting feelings, using this and other exercises and that they use the adage 'accept the feeling; choose the action' to avoid conflict both within and outside their relationship.

Session 6

Steve and Laura had experimented with accepting their feelings and using the adage 'accept the feeling; choose the action' to avoid conflict.

Steve gave an example of having focused on and accepted his feelings of irritation when he'd felt controlled by Laura. He'd chosen to withhold any negative comment, Paccepted the situation (on the basis that Laura had done the only thing she could have done at the time) and had mentioned it to her at a later opportunity, using an 'I statement'.

Laura gave an example of having accepted angry feelings when one of their children was playing up. She chose not to follow her normal pattern of chastising him, waited instead for him to calm down while she Paccepted the situation, based on determinist thinking, then spoke calmly about her need for him to do as she asked.

We devoted the balance of this session to covering some more AAT techniques, including owning our reactions, taking responsibility for both sides of an interaction (on the basis that the other person is doing the only thing they could be doing in the absence of any input from someone else), taking responsibility for our experience and Paccepting it all.

We agreed the next session would be the last as our goals had been achieved.

Session 7

Steve and Laura confirmed their relationship and prospects for the future had greatly improved.

They believed they were using all the AAT tools they'd learned. Laura particularly liked 'owning reactions'. She said it had changed the way she dealt with challenging interactions, enabling her to immediately Paccept the situation and take control of her response.

Steve described an experience of taking responsibility for both sides of a challenging interaction at work when he realised the other person was doing the only thing he could have been doing at the time. Steve was again able to Paccept the situation and focus only on how he could best influence the other person's awareness.

I used the balance of the session to outline some more power tools covered in my web-based 'Positive Mind Training'.

15.

Worry

Jane was a worrier. She worried about whether her children would succeed at school, whether they were happy and whether they would make their way in the world. She worried about whether her husband might lose his job and whether she might lose him. She worried about her sister's recent cancer scare and whether it might return. And when her dog wandered off with his neighbourhood friends as he was prone to do, she worried whether he would return safely, as of course he always did.

There was a lot more that Jane found to worry about.

Session 1

Once I'd heard her story, I asked Jane whether anything she'd ever worried about had actually happened. She said she thought something probably had but couldn't think of anything right now. She had the good humour to suggest that if she worried enough, a coincidence would ensure she'd get it right eventually.

She knew her excessive worrying was irrational, at least with the benefit of hindsight. She just needed a means to stop.

I told her I was going to teach her a way of thinking that would not appear to immediately address her worrying but that we'd extend it to deal with worry later. I told her about 'accepting what is' and the technique of Positive Acceptance (Pacceptance), employing the justification that it makes no sense to wish things were already different.

I asked her to practice this way of thinking through the following week and told her that in the next session we'd extend the technique so it could be applied to the future and stop her worrying.

I also told her about accepting uncomfortable feelings, pointing out that she may sometimes need to accept her feelings until they'd subsided sufficiently for her to be able to use Pacceptance.

I gave her the shower exercise (see Chapter 3 after the table) to practice at home. Otherwise her goal was to spend the week practicing Pacceptance and accepting any uncomfortable feelings.

Session 2

Jane had been using Pacceptance every day and said she loved it. She said it had already reduced her worrying. There had been several occasions when she realised her worrying thoughts involved wishing something were already different.

For example one of her children was spending the night with a friend and she was worrying whether everything was going to be alright, whether the family were reliable and so on. She realised she was effectively wishing the situation didn't exist, which was wishing something were already different. Realising that this was wishing for the impossible, she dropped the thought and refocused on what she could do to make things better. She called the family to check everything was OK.

I then told her how we could extend Pacceptance to apply it to the future. I explained that whenever we're worrying, we're wanting something to be different in the future from the way we think it might be **and** we don't believe we can control it.

Wanting something to be different in the future that we believe we cannot control is about as irrational as wanting the past to be different. Realising this, we can drop the thought and refocus on what we can do, if anything, to take more control of whatever we were worrying about or, if we cannot get control, accept whatever will be.

I mentioned the song 'Que sera sera …. whatever will be will be'. Jane was familiar with the song but, until now, had never recognised the wisdom it contained. As she thought about the title, she recognised the power of this way of thinking. She stated her determination to adopt this way of thinking all the time. She agreed that when she found herself worrying, she would think about the song title and let go of the worrying thought.

If the worrying thought was particularly negative, rather than just accepting that the future would be OK, she agreed to combine this with the additional tool of recognising that her worry was almost certainly exaggerated, either in the likelihood of something bad happening, or the consequences even if it did happen, or both.

Jane recognised that the prime AAT tool was little different to what she'd already been doing in Paccepting the past and present. The key was to recognise the worrying thought was irrational, drop it and refocus on what she could do to take more control.

We practiced the technique in-session and she agreed to continue it at home.

Session 3

Jane had enjoyed significant success with applying the Pacceptance idea to the future. She said she wasn't thinking too much about why the thought was irrational. She wasn't bothering too much about whether she was wishing the past, present or future were different. She was just dropping negative thoughts and refocusing on whether there was anything she could do to improve the future.

She hadn't had any worrying thoughts negative enough to warrant using the exaggeration tool. But she confirmed she would keep this in mind if she encountered any particularly negative worries.

I gave her another AAT worry tool. I told her that once she became practiced at Pacceptance, she would know that whatever happens in the future she'll be able to Paccept it.

We ended at that point. Jane was confident she had all the tools she needed to keep her worrying under control.

16.

Evidence and Research

If you've started using AAT tools in your own life or as a therapist, you'll already be aware of the benefits. If you haven't, then hopefully you can sense it from the cases outlined in this book.

Testimonials for the 'development training' equivalent of AAT (Acceptance Action Training ... taught on the web via a webinar-based training called Positive Mind Training) can be found at www.abicord. com/testimonials.

Feedback from Positive Mind Training participants has been dramatic. We've asked participants to measure their life satisfaction and effectiveness before and after the training on a simple 0 to 10 scale, where 10 is the most satisfied and effective person they can imagine. We've had numerous participants report changes from 3 to 10 and some from 2 to 9. Most change from 6, 7, 8 or 9 to 9 or 10. Subsequent reviews have shown that changes have been sustained or further improved (measured in groups as feedback is anonymous).

In my own life and my own experience as a therapist, the impact has also been dramatic. If only three basic AAT tools of accepting feelings, 'accept the feeling; choose the action' and 'accepting what is', including 'determinist thinking', are added to an existing therapy, such as CBT, the benefits for clients are major and immediate.

Further research is underway. Initial results of comparing CBT alone versus AAT alone show major differences (I avoid the term 'significant' as anyone familiar with statistics will know this term is pretty meaningless when trying to assess the scale of any difference). The number of sessions to resolve common issues including anxiety-based issues (such as panic, phobias, social anxiety, public speaking anxiety and OCD), depression, addictions, self-harm, anger problems, worry, confidence issues, relationship issues, family issues and weight management are greatly reduced. Where results are measurable, effectiveness has dramatically improved.

Where this has been tested, sustainability has also substantially improved. This includes dramatic results for smoking cessations (99% successful on a sustained basis) and weight loss (95% on a sustained basis). Other approaches are typically substantially less than 50% for sustained smoking cessation and below 10% for sustained weight loss.

Reduction in the number of sessions to achieve resolution enables more sessions to be devoted to Acceptance Action Training (coaching and self-development) techniques, covered in my web-based Positive Mind Training.

Any therapist can use AAT tools, alone or in conjunction with another therapy, and observe the benefits for themselves. Introducing the tools to a few clients would normally be sufficient to indicate the impact and provide strong encouragement to continue.

We're seeking therapists to participate in further research. If you're interested, please contact us via the contact page on Abicord's website or email enquiries@ abicord.com. Free AAT training will be provided to participants.

17.

Conclusions and Future Plans

The case studies included in this book are just a sample of how AAT can be applied in specific cases. AAT can be used effectively for any issue, psychological or otherwise.

Bipolar disorder, self-harm, insomnia, procrastination, eating disorders, smoking cessation and weight issues are some of the other psychological issues where AAT has been effectively employed beyond the examples provided in this book.

Research carried out to date has demonstrated highly effective, rapid and sustained results from AAT compared to other therapies.

AAT can be used alone or in combination with CBT or other therapies.

A summary of the AAT tools covered in this book is provided at the end of the book for ease of reference.

Abicord offers regular Positive Mind Training via webinars. While these are development trainings, they're equally applicable to Acceptance Action Therapy for therapists. The webinar-based trainings also include tools, primarily development tools, not covered in this book.

A stand-alone Positive Mind Training webinar, accessible through Abicord's website, is free to readers of this book at www.positive-mind-training.com. Thanks to the involvement of a wealthy sponsor, the full training is now also free to the vast majority of participants.

Further trainings for therapists, coaches and clients, that build on the Positive Mind Training webinars and this book, are available on Abicord's website. See www.abicord.com/further-opportunities. In the case of therapists, all these trainings contribute to CPD (Continuous Professional Development) requirements.

Weight Loss and Smoking Cessation programmes, using AAT and other tools, are also available on that website. These have been so successful, they're now guaranteed (a one year, money-back guarantee for achieving the goal and sustaining it).

Services for corporates and other organisations, using AAT and Positive Mind Training principles, are available from Abicord Consulting. They can be found at www.abicordconsulting.co.uk

We'd be happy to hear from therapists who adopt AAT in the treatment of their clients. We're always looking for experiences and ideas for improving the content and application of AAT. Please contact us via the contact page on Abicord's website or email enquiries@abicord.com.

A free forum (facebook group) called 'Amazing Lives For All' has been created for readers of this book and graduates of the 'Positive Mind Training' Intro webinar, to share experiences and learn more. You can join this free forum at www.facebook.com/groups/amazinglivesforall

If you'd like to see, or speak to, a qualified AAT therapist, or acceptance action coach or trainer, you can find one at the Association for Acceptance Action Coaching, Therapy and Training (AAACTT). See www.aaactt.com. Therapists, coaches and trainers can also refer to this site to see how to qualify as an Acceptance Action Therapist, Coach or Trainer and join the 'Find an Acceptance Action Therapist, Coach or Trainer' service.

A separate forum (another facebook group), called 'PMT Graduates', has been created for graduates of the full 'Positive Mind Training' webinar-based programme or equivalent seminar-based programmes. This forum provides PMT Graduates, including acceptance action therapists, coaches and trainers, an opportunity to share experiences, obtain further training and participate in a major project to spread Acceptance Action Training. The goals of this project are to:

- Provide Acceptance Action Training (the full 'Positive Mind Training' webinar-based programme or equivalent seminar-based programmes) to 1 billion people in the next five years
- Change the way the world thinks
- Resolve major conflicts
- Achieve and sustain all weight goals
- Provide further opportunities to attendees of

our trainings

- Fund substantial, well-known charities to end poverty and provide other benefits that trainings alone cannot provide.

As a contribution to the last goal, all net revenues from the trainings, the association, forums and sales of this book will be passed on to charities.

Access to the 'PMT Graduates' forum is provided on completion of the full 'Positive Mind Training' webinar-based programme or equivalent seminar-based programmes.

Here's wishing you every success in the application of Acceptance Action principles, as a therapy (AAT) to address any mind-based issues, a development training through the 'Positive Mind Training' programme and, for therapists, coaches and trainers, in your practice as a highly effective treatment or training for your clients.

AAT Tools Summary

- Paccept what is (including what was) at every opportunity
- Stop worrying: apply Pacceptance to the future (whatever will be will be) to the extent we cannot control it. Recognize that whatever happens we'll be able to Paccept it
- For major worries, add recognising exaggerations in probability or consequence
- Recognise we and others have always done the only thing we could have done, given who we were at the time
- Paccept our own past actions and the past and present actions of others
- The future is wide open to create whatever we wish for
- Accept ourselves totally as we are (we're the only person we could have been right now), at the same time as seeking to develop
- 'Accept for now' any uncomfortable feelings (fully experience and accept them). Ask the '3 questions'.
- 'Accept the feeling, choose the (opposite)

action to unwind unconscious beliefs driving recurring unproductive feelings and behaviours

- Own our reactions (we can then view our reaction and the trigger separately and Paccept both)
- Recognise others believe they're right and reasonable just as we do. Try to understand their perspective and develop compromise or win-win solutions
- Take responsibility for the other person's behaviour in our interactions (the other person is doing the only thing they could be doing, given who they are right now, unless we intervene)
- Reconcile with significant others where needed
- Take responsibility for the way we experience every moment; then choose our experience using AAT tools
- Recognise nothing that's ever happened, nor any situation that exists right now, could have been different, so Paccept it all
- Accept the feeling, choose the action, challenge the thought
- We can often let go of residual uncomfortable feelings once we've fully accepted them
- Use the further 'power tools', outlined in my web-based Positive Mind Training, to take control of the future

Printed in Great Britain
by Amazon